Thin Lines:
A Vineyard Journey

Thin Lines:
A Vineyard Journey

John Pryor Fulkerson

ISBN: 1542895146
ISBN 13: 9781542895149
Library of Congress Control Number: 2017901664
CreateSpace Independent Publishing Platform
North Charleston, South Carolina

Dedicated to Lynn, my wife and best friend.
Special thanks to Lynn for her thoughtful recommendations and for the cover art,
and thanks also to my good friends
Ted McMahon and Jerry Geci
for their guidance in writing this little book.

Prologue

Upon gazing at the stars, the ocean, or a work of art, one may be so moved by beauty as to experience a sense of connection and truth. The ancient Greeks called this truth *aletheia*. Japanese Zen Buddhists define this enlightenment as *satori or kensha*. Such beauty and connectedness may be found in nature, music, poetry, or … in a glass of fine wine. The art of grape growers and wine makers is to reveal the beautiful inner truth of grapes in wine.

In wine making, all the factors that go into it, from preparation of the soil to the grape harvest to the final product, must coordinate in order to uncover the best and most beautiful essence of grapes in wine. The grape grower's art is to provide an optimal environment for grapes to grow and represent their potential. The vintner's challenge is to then reveal the beauty of grapes in a glass of wine.

Our sleeping aesthetic
and communion beyond bread and wine
are far from mortality's call
on paths through vineyards, streams, gardens, and flowering fields.

THE SEED

The ancient Tain-l'Hermitage vineyard, with its well-tended old vines and storybook landscape, rose out of parting clouds as we drove along the Rhone River of France in the fall of 1998. We were fortunate to find a good, small hotel, where we checked in along with our friends Jay and Nancy. Our rooms looked out directly across the Rhone to the magnificent l'Hermitage vineyard, where we had bought some wine that morning. The name Jaboulet, a wine maker well known for producing fine Rhone wines, was prominent on that hillside, where grape vines seemed to weave into a distant azure sky.

Beauty, mystery, chemistry, and biology surround grapes and wine. Seeing those well-tended vineyards and later entering the half-lit caves of wineries in the Rhone region reminded me of how the wine we drink carries us to such places. For some, a glass of wine is a vicarious journey, made possible by a nostalgic sense of the wine's place of origin. This happened to us months later, at our home in the rolling hills of northwest Connecticut, when we opened our bottle of wine from l'Hermitage. Even letting the wine breathe after extracting the cork brought back memories of the Rhone valley's waving vines, drenched with sunlight far above the churning river below.

Later that evening, after Lynn and I had been carried back in time, I thought about growing grapes around our home in Connecticut. Several vineyards flourished near us in the northwest hills of our state, making the thought tangible. Might we capture the character of our home—its glacial till soil, crisp mornings, cool climate, rolling hills, and clear air—in grapes and wine?

The decision to grow grapes came quickly and easily—so easily that I now reflect, years later, about the factors leading to such a monumental shift of direction and focus in life.

In medical school, I had been moved by Lewis Thomas's book *Lives of a Cell* (1). In this gem of a book, Thomas glorifies the cellular and biologic intricacies that make life, in all its amazing and diverse forms, possible. He simplifies and brings excitement to the everyday cellular interactions that create our life experience. Here are a few exemplary passages from *Lives of a Cell*: "Most of the associations between living things we know about are essentially cooperative ones, symbolic in one way or another. We do not have solitary beings. Every creature is, in some sense, connected to and dependent on the rest." And:

> "We all engage in a very personal, interdependent, yet largely unknowing way with the dynamic biologic phenomena, large and small, which are so inherent in life."

The cellular biology, physiology, genetics, embryology, chemistry, and human anatomy I studied in medical school made Lewis Thomas's words resonate in my ears. Our lives are blessings of biology and chemistry in a world of miraculous and beautiful natural interactions.

Each living cell
is awake in its unique ancestral call—
naked splendor
hidden from human eyes
in its complex, silent world.

Growing grapes and making wine seemed like a profound way to interact with the "dynamic biologic phenomena" that Lewis Thomas described so well. I wanted to learn how to interact with grape vines and their fruit—to capture, in scent and taste, the environment in which grapes are raised, to enable their inner cellular machinery to perform at its very best to produce good wine. I also realized that my desire to grow grapes and make wine had been inspired by some very special physicians I had known—more on that later.

A little wine maker's supply shop was located only a few miles from our Connecticut home. Actually, it was the back-room operation of a furniture store, run by a couple who also made wine; a dimly lit, cave-like area behind an old iron gate at the back of the main store. The proprietress would usually sit in the back, during the somewhat unpredictable times that they were open, and she would emerge when anyone entered the furniture-store entrance, located inconspicuously at the far end of a car-dealership parking lot. This place had the feel of a privileged inner sanctum.

Chemicals on the shelves, large containers for making and storing wine, air-lock devices, pipettes, and unusual glass containers were surrounded by pictures of distant vineyards and technical books on wine making. This alluring place, still open over fifteen years later as I write this story, provided tools and supplies for making wine. The chemicals, including pectic enzyme, organic acids, and sodium hydroxide, reminded me of premedical organic chemistry and medical-school biochemistry classes. The shop's high shelves displayed the variety of flasks, corks, tubing, and instruments that are necessary to measure sugar and acid concentrations in wine and to ultimately promote the transformation of grape juice into wine. My confidence grew as I recognized how familiar I was with these tools of chemistry and that making wine was simply basic applied organic chemistry, biochemistry really—courses required for all physicians. I purchased two books: one on growing grapes and one on making wine.

I was determined to grow grapes *without* using insecticides, which would disrupt the natural balance of the vineyard by killing both helpful and detrimental insects. Insecticides would also threaten birds, which control the insect population, and leave residue, traces of which would likely end up in the final wine. A healthy, natural environment would favor optimal grapes and pure wine.

Choosing the right grape varieties, available commercially as grape roots (or "rootstock"), that would grow well and produce good grapes in our cool Connecticut environment would be the first important challenge. The *Vitis vinifera* grape varieties cabernet sauvignon, cabernet franc, chardonnay, petit syrah (shiraz), sangiovese, pinot noir, merlot, Riesling, zinfandel, sauvignon blanc, and gewürztraminer grapes were perhaps the best known and popular. *Vitis vinifera* grapes are known to be excellent for making wine but grow best in warm, temperate climates with long growing seasons, such as southern Europe, Chile, California, Australia, northern New Zealand, and South Africa. They also tend to produce wine with fairly distinct olfactory, visual, and gustatory characteristics unique to their genetic makeup. The wine maker may reveal, embellish, or ruin these potentially beautiful qualities.

Vitis vinifera grapes originated in the Near East and western Mediterranean, according to Arroyo-Garcia in his study of grape chloroplast DNA (2). They grew well for centuries around the Mediterranean, particularly in France, until a little insect called phylloxera was introduced inadvertently from America to Europe, particularly to France, in the late nineteenth century. These tiny aphids suck sap specifically out of *vinifera* roots, eventually weakening and killing *vinifera* grape vines. This created havoc among growers of *Vitis vinifera* worldwide as the production of fine grapes and wine plummeted as a result of this unfortunate infestation.

The roots of native grapes in North America are resistant to phylloxera, so J. E. Planchon and Charles Riley grafted phylloxera-prone *vinifera* vines onto American grapevine roots. This solution subsequently worked out nicely on both sides of the Atlantic, so European *vinifera* became commercially available on American rootstock. European vineyards were replanted with *vinifera* grafted to American roots in order to thwart deadly, root-damaging phyllox-era. Additionally, native North American rootstock tolerates the cold far better than *vinifera*.

I wondered if *vinifera* grafted onto hardy rootstock could withstand the sometimes fiercely cold winters of the northwest Connecticut hills where we would plant our vines.

7:00 a.m.

It's 7:00 a.m., and the woodstove warms its little room.
Last night's full moon eases silently from the frozen landscape
As the furnace drones against chill air, and the Teakettle whistles.

Evening

It's evening now, and the incandescent last sun
and ceramic-blue January sky
reflect from vintage glass
in the darkening town
where coffeehouse lamps
once punctuated old red brick
and blessed the frigid winter air.

As I sought to understand how to grow grapes in our northern climate, I found that vintners in Upstate New York, near Lake Seneca, were mastering cold-weather viticulture. One in particular had developed expansive vineyards there, where he produced several excellent wines from grafted *vinifera* grapes in the snow belt of Upstate New York. He was considered to be an expert on growing *vinifera* in cool climates. I called him.

This man's knowledge, confidence, and generous advice convinced me that I could grow *vinifera* grapes in northwest Connecticut, so I put in an order for chardonnay, cabernet franc, gewürztraminer, and Riesling—to be delivered in early May 1999. Reading about the process of growing grapes and making wine was my daily commitment for several weeks, while local commercial grape growers provided eager encouragement. I decided to join the Connecticut Vineyard and Winery Association.

Our proposed vineyard site faced a little east of south and therefore was oriented well for maximal sun exposure. The meadow ran down to a half-acre pond, a source of relative warmth for our vineyard on cold nights, as its mildly warmed air would slide up through the meadow during colder parts of the year. Study of the slope during winter months revealed that frost disappeared a little earlier toward the top of the slope than at the bottom. The slope would allow good drainage, and erosion would not be a problem since the pitch of the slope was quite gentle, with a well-established hayfield all around.

Bob, a local farmer, had helped us from time to time with our farming efforts, whether we were growing vegetables, chopping wood, doing tractor chores, weeding, performing equipment maintenance, mowing hay, putting up fences, painting, or spreading manure. Sometimes he would appear at our door singing a Willie Nelson song ("Blue Skies" was a favorite). We had coffee together whenever possible, and would generally stir up some lively banter. Bob could handle just about anything related to farming. Not one for sunscreen or shorts, he would work through the hottest summer days in long pants, often with no hat. In Bob's mind, stacking wood was not a task that

9

required gloves, despite the fact that he had had major hand surgery a few years before. His hands were sturdy. He had survived a ruptured bowel and came back as strong as ever after spending most of one summer in a hospital with several trips to the operating room. A bout of sudden eye pain turned out to be a detached retina (he thought it was a beesting), which took most of the vision from one of his eyes. At one point, he had his back fused and was ready to work a few weeks later. Bob kept on singing and working. His work was very episodic for us, so while we didn't see him a lot, he was always there when we needed a hand. Then, at the end of a day's work, he would walk to his car, and on would go Willie Nelson.

Dirt

First loved as a mud ball in childhood,
now respected and enriched with aged manure,
to grow our peas and lettuce,
grapes and raspberries,
woolen earth, rich in vitamins,
for some lucky earthworm
just trying to find its way—
no eyes, just a hankering for dirt
like me.

We created five rows in the vineyard, enough room for twenty-five vines in each row. Preparing the soil properly was critical for growing grapes successfully, and this had to be done before the grapes arrived.

The dirt, or soil, in which we grow things is a dynamic layer on the surface of the earth, combining shattered bedrock with other materials brought in by wind, rain, migration, earthworms, and water flow to form the substance with which we are familiar and from which so many good things grow. Organic materials mixed in are constantly transformed by microorganisms, of which there may be almost one million different types in one gram of soil, making it the "most abundant ecosystem in the world" according to Jon Copley (3).

In a healthy, sustainable environment, soil is brimming with life—bugs, worms, bacteria, mold, and other tiny creatures that work and rework the soil, using what they need and adding their own nutrients back to it. Soil makes life possible; it provides grains, grass, vegetables, trees, and fruits to nourish creatures like us while it processes carbon dioxide to produce oxygen. Respect for soil is respect for life at a basic level. We owe our lives to it.

"Contrast our attitude towards soil as a commodity with the attitude of Scripture: Cain's punishment was to be banished from the soil he loved. The Psalmist loves the very dust of Jerusalem, and the Promised Land is also described as soil. It is a gift from God, to be nurtured for abundance(4)."

This blessed soil relates to the French word for soil, which is *terre*. From *terre* evolved the term "terroir," a much more encompassing word that includes the overall environment of a location. Terroir includes the soil, climate, local yeasts, and subtleties of a place that will profoundly affect the grapes and other plants grown there. Of these factors, soil is the greatest factor, as it is the primary reservoir of water and nutrition for grapes. Soil is mysterious, a subject of study at academic institutions devoted to agriculture. Although we know that balanced acidity and availability of nutrients in the soil are necessary in order to grow healthy grapes, there is little doubt that unknown factors, beyond texture and composition of soil, have an impact on the flavor and other characteristics of fruits and vegetables that grow in a particular place. This is why wine made from a specific grape species will yield an endless variety of subtle tastes and scents when grown in different soils and unique terroirs.

Vintners care deeply about the soil from which their grapes come, as it is at the heart of their winemaking process. Soil mysteriously conveys a "sense of place" to the wine that comes from its grapes. This is reproducible, to a large extent, from year to year when the winemaking technique is the same, using grapes from the same terroir. Cabernet sauvignon wine made from grapes grown in Bordeaux is reproducibly distinct from wine made with cabernet sauvignon grapes grown in Sonoma, California. Yet even so, each year is uniquely different from every other year, resulting in "good years" and "bad years" for vintages of specific grapes grown in the same vineyard. In one broad sense, the goodness and beauty of a year's harvest is at the mercy of that year's terroir. The soil itself; the environment of that year; and how well the soil, wind, rain, and the human factors (such as pruning, watering, weed control, etc.) interplay with intangibles make each year a new, challenging, and exciting mystery.

Fortunately, the fall of 1998 had been warm, and this helped us get our soil tilled and prepared for the spring 1999 planting. A few initial soil samples taken from the upper and lower aspects of the vineyard revealed very acid soil, with pHs between 5.4 and 5.6 (7.0 is neutral on a scale ranging up to 14; below 7.0 is increasingly acid, and above 7.0 increasingly alkaline). Our soil was lacking optimal amounts of a few important nutrients, including nitrogen, potassium, and magnesium, so some modification and enrichment were necessary. I had previously assumed that great grapes, and subsequently great wine, came from rich soil. Surprisingly, though, this is not how it works. Some plants, such as blueberries, like acidity. Others, like beans and peppers, like alkalinity. After reading some Cornell University publications on grape growing, I learned what I could about soils of places that grow grapes successfully. The gravelly soil of Bordeaux, a gift from the Gironde River estuary to Bordeaux's grape growers and wine makers, is not the rich, loamy, dark earth that one might expect, but it is well suited to grow grapes—particularly cabernet sauvignon and merlot. And the soil there, like that along the Rhine River in Germany where some fine Riesling grows, has plenty of limestone, which is alkaline, thereby raising the pH and making the soil less acid. Grapes can like soil that doesn't appeal as much to some other plants, such as grass. Looking back at our meadows, the relatively sparse hay was mixed with acid-loving wild strawberries, ferns, and huckleberries, further confirming that our soil was acidic. But top-quality grapes depend on optimal soil acidity (not too acid) to maximally absorb micronutrients such as aluminum, magnesium, calcium, boron, and many other trace elements that add to the flavor and character of a wine. So it is not just the presence of these elements in the soil, it is how they are absorbed, and this is based to a large extent on balanced soil acidity. One might think that this is all well worked out. A report on our soil from the University of Connecticut revealed that our soil pH (acidity) was suitable for grapes. Looking into this further, however, I found in studies from Cornell University that a pH of 6.0–6.2 (still acid, but less so) is better for growing grapes than our pH, 5.4–5.6. I concluded that our soil was too acid to produce optimal grapes. With a slightly higher pH (less acidity), our grape plants would be better able to absorb key elements from the soil, according to experts on this topic at Cornell. Too much cane (the leggy branches of the grapevines) might result from poor acidity, and this would reduce fruit production. Optimizing soil acidity would be important to the quality of our future wine. Additionally, different soils and acidities are better for some grape varieties than others! The goal was to grow the best grapes possible for our location, and then make the best possible wine from those grapes, but we didn't know what would grow well in our soil, yet.

Adjusting soil was different than the precision I had learned in medical-school chemistry and in my career as a surgeon. Soil adjustment is a game of approximations—more like cooking—in which one must know the ingredients and then mix them in optimal proportions, to produce the best possible result. One priority was adding organic matter, with its assorted micronutrients and elements, at the front end, before our grapes were placed in the ground. The other was getting the acidity of our soil as close as possible to a target 6.0–6.2 pH in the fall of 1998, so that it would be ready for a May 1999 initial planting.

Manure was the most mysterious of what we added to our soil, as amounts of specific elements and nutrients were not listed on a side panel. We call it "brown gold." The beauty of manure (aged manure is best), however, is that it tends to be chock full of nutrients and, particularly in our rural area, is pretty cheap (later I was able to exchange some of my wine for deliveries of manure). I called my friend Paul, who had access to good manure, and within a matter of days, we had a dump-truck load (several tons) of well-aged cow poo in our back yard. The spreading of it started before the frost got too dense. For the five rows, though, I couldn't use all of it, so about half went into a stockpile for future use. A fair portion also went in Lynn's organic vegetable garden.

Next were the other nutrients—limestone, green sand, and phosphate on top of the manure, yielding three rows ready before a dense frost blanketed the meadows. The new soil blend was tilled thoroughly to be as optimal as possible for spring planting. Then frost turned to ice, the manure pile became rock solid, and soil preparation was finished by December 1, 1998.

Inspiration

My father was strong and loyal:
a scholar, a friend, a light,
a reason to learn, to emulate and endure,
to honor, grow and yield good fruit.

Several grape growers and vintners, who were successfully raising grapes and making wine in Connecticut, were generous with their guidance and encouragement. I became intrigued by the somewhat unusual grape types (varietals) they grew—Cayuga, Vidal blanc, seyval blanc, Marechal Foch, and cabernet franc—and I was given samples of their best to taste (note that some grape names are capitalized and others are not- only those named for a specific person or place are capitalized). Much to my surprise and delight, the less known, cold-weather hardy grapes produced unique and enjoyable wines in the hands of these master northern-climate growers/vintners. A new world of scent and taste in wine was unfolding before me in grapes that would grow well where we lived.

My inspiration grew upon the discovery of these exciting new grape varietals, the dedication and delight of those involved in the cultivation of grapes and wine, the predictable renewal of a vineyard every year as it becomes robust again with new life—and so on, year after year. I thought of my aunt Elisabeth's husband, Currier, who cultivated and hybridized daylilies and irises, delighting in the return of his "children" every year.

I had always admired this man of great humor, love of life, passion, and integrity, whom I had first met when I was a young child and went with my parents to visit with Currier at Seaways, his family home on the Maine coast, where lobster from a local lobsterman (his dear friend, as was almost everyone there, it seemed) was a late-day celebratory event whenever we were there. We all helped prepare the lobsters, boiling them in a huge pot on his stove after "anesthetizing them" in his freezer for about a half hour, and they were always, always "the best lobster I've ever had!" according to Uncle Currier, whose enthusiasm was genuine and whose laughter was heartfelt. Newspapers were spread on the dining table in his living room overlooking Casco Bay, with a distant view of Admiral Robert Peary's home on Eagle Island. Peary was the first explorer to reach the North Pole. From the perspective of a young boy, Currier's home expressed the intrigue and otherworldly exploratory energy that were so much a part of Robert Peary, the sea, and the childhood stories of Peary's bravery and conquest as he explored the Arctic, before returning to his Eagle Island home. Perhaps it was the palpable tenacity and will to engage in the challenges of life that made these two great men—Currier and Robert Peary—so admirable to a young boy in the late 1950s and early 1960s, even as the Beatles and the Beach Boys played their soulful tunes on car radios. Nonetheless, one of the best parts of time spent at Seaways was Currier's frequent and hearty laughter.

Uncle Currier told tales of his life—the cabin he had built with his son; the sailing regattas he had won in his beloved boat, Seminole; his experiences hybridizing flowers; his many friends; his father's struggle with psoriatic arthritis; and his challenges as dean of New York University (NYU) Medical School. Later in life, until he died at age 102, every day was a challenge as he struggled with his own severely deformed, arthritic knees. Nonetheless, his days were filled with eager engagement in the natural world, as he pursued his passion for hybridizing flowers at his beloved home. He would go out to his flowers with a walker, drop to the ground to work with his flowers, and then slowly, painfully climb back up to the walker and move a few steps farther. All his gardening tools were attached to the walker. I never heard him complain.

Currier had married my aunt Elisabeth after his first wife died in an automobile accident. For Elisabeth, this was a first marriage at age sixty-seven. Currier was about ten years older than she was at that time. They cared beautifully for each other in their later years. Aunt Elisabeth, a lovely, loving, altruistic teetotaler, would intervene in Currier's traditional late-afternoon martini with a pot of tea on a little tray with some peanuts or cheese and crackers. He would respectfully accept the tray, abandoning the martini (for a while), and they would have tea together, every day.

Currier was a powerful role model; he immersed himself in whatever he was doing, entering a quiet solitude among his beloved daylilies and irises. Yet he loved people, particularly when they were interested in his flowers. He read a lot and could talk on many topics. He loved a scholarly debate and was a natural storyteller who enthralled me as a child. I couldn't fathom combining the genetic materials of two different flowers to produce a completely new flower with attributes of the two parents. This was a miracle, to be sure. Later, as I struggled through biology and chemistry in college, with courses in plant biology and genetics, the hybridization process became clearer to me. Currier mentioned colchicine, which he had used to treat patients with gout in his career as a rheumatologist, and that he later applied it to daylily seeds to arrest their chromosomes into a "tetraploid" state, such that they would then produce special, genetically endowed super daylilies—much larger than usual because they had double the normal amounts of genetic material. This scientific discovery was revolutionary and placed Currier at the forefront of the daylily world.

After having created and "named" a number of award winning daylilies, he moved on to Japanese irises and introduced some irises that are still sold and planted in gardens around the world today. While traveling several years ago, we were delighted to find Currier's daylilies in the Sydney, Australia Botanical Gardens.

Once, a camera crew from Martha Stewart's magazine showed up at Currier's house in Maine. He hadn't known who she was, but was happy that someone wanted to photograph and write about his flowers. The magazine published a lengthy article about his life dedicated to daylilies and irises, with flattering pictures of him with his loving smile among his beloved flowers on the coast of Maine. His admirable life as dean of NYU Medical School had faded into the distant past as his beautiful uniquely hybridized flowers took center stage.

Not only did this fine man raise flowers, he gave of his time to care for my aunt's disabled niece, Margaret, who was severely afflicted by cerebral palsy. She suffered with a back deformity, walked awkwardly, and had great difficulty communicating. Her voice had a squawking, shrill tone, and as a child, I had great difficulty understanding her. She loved Uncle Currier, who would single-handedly help this unfortunate woman up and down the steep stairs at their home, despite her deformity and weakness and his bowed, painful knees. Currier's life devoted to others—Margaret, Elisabeth, his children, his patients, and his flowers— brought him consistent happiness and beauty.

Currier's knack for engaging with the earth, while sharing his abundant appreciation of flowers with others, was appealing and powerful in my eventual decision to grow grapes and make wine. The fact that I had trained in the sciences, just like Currier, made growing things tangible for me. In addition to understanding animal life, premedical studies required understanding all life, including plants and their adversaries in the biologic world—bugs, mildew, birds, and other creatures. I knew I would find great adventure and joy in the production of grapes and in the sharing of their wine, much as Currier had relished the growing of irises and daylilies, whose beauty he would then share with others. My decision and conviction to grow grapes came most directly from Currier McEwen.

Thin Places

From Mindle Burgoyne's *Walking through Thin Places*: "Thin places are ports in the storm of life where pilgrims can move closer to the God they seek, where one leaves that which is familiar and journeys into the Divine Presence. They are stopping places where men and women are given pause to wonder what lies beyond the mundane rituals, grief, trials and boredom of their daily lives. They probe to the core of the human heart and open a path that leads to satisfying the familiar hungers and yearnings common to all people on earth, the hunger to be connected, to be part of something greater, to be loved, to find peace."

Many in our Western civilization consider the small island of Iona, in the Scottish Inner Hebrides, a thin place. Its simplicity, wildness, rugged coast, surrounding ocean, ancient stone-monastery vestiges, remoteness, and Celtic history all pertain to its thinness. As one comes close to the border of earth and heaven, one may enter a thin place. Thin places tend to bring us into connection with the vastness of existence and all creation. Iona has brought many to an awareness of the Divine in and around them.

Thin Places

I thought about Iona,
a Scottish island
that's thin
and just across the Atlantic
from where I was that day
on the Isles of Shoals,
New Hampshire.

Thin places are Narnian doors
that connect heaven and earth
(which are three feet apart,
the Celts say).

I listened to a gull
above the percussive surf,
tall Timothy grass and blue sky
between us,
a stone cottage
merging with the rocky shore,

and thought,
Yes—three feet.

The Rhone valley, Lewis Thomas's book, the hills around my home, the Isles of Shoals, and my vineyard all seem thin to me. Currier's coastal Maine home was thin. Perhaps when Currier engaged with his flowers, the crashing ocean nearby, the breezes, the salt air, the cliff rose, the high grass, and Eagle Island surrounding those moments, heaven and earth merged. Getting close to the eternal was how it seemed—our smallness integrated in some important way with the vastness around. There are many elements leading to thinness—wildness, vulnerability, passion, contrast, integrity, love, compassion, connection, vastness, and peace, to name a few.

Posts and Wires

The winter months of 1999 allowed me time to study viticulture while considering which grape varieties to plant the following spring. I had to try growing *vinifera* grapes (chardonnay, cabernet franc, gewürztraminer, and riesling), despite the evident success of local growers with French-American hybrids. Phone calls to several grapevine distributors revealed that obtaining rootstock of the most desirable *vinifera* grape varieties by early May might be difficult. Fortunately, one grower had a good supply of *vinifera* and could ship 125 vines in May 1999. The chosen grape varieties grew well in Upstate New York and would flourish, it seemed, in Connecticut. So the order went in for all four varieties of *vinifera* that had been grafted onto hardy, phylloxera-resistant 3309 rootstock.

In March 1999, the south side of our manure pile began to soften, sending off billows of steam as organic processes began to churn, ripening our "brown gold." We did some additional spreading of manure through the rows, and we saved some to place around each vine that would be planted in May. After tilling the soil again, we sent new samples of soil for testing at the University of Connecticut, and reports came back showing that we had substantially reduced the soil acidity. In fact, if anything, the pH was a little bit on the high side (too little acidity) and was approaching neutral pH (7.0). As the alkalinizing lime would wash deeper into the soil, the target pH of 6.0–6.2 would be attained, settling between the extreme acidity of the original soil test and the neutrality, or relatively low-acidity soil, created by my zealous initial lime application.

Momentum gathered: the rows looked good, all tilled with manure and nutrients, the soil had been analyzed, and I had ordered the grapevines. Getting the vineyard set, though, required far more work.

Vineyard posts must last a long time. Red cedar is durable and stands up well. White-pine posts are cheaper, but red-cedar ones endure many more years and look good too. Locust provides durability that surpasses almost all other types of wood, so the choice became red cedar for the end posts, as they are aesthetically nicer to look at, with locust in between, twelve feet apart. In New England, one must place posts at least three feet into the ground, below frost level, to prevent shifting from the vagaries of the harsh Connecticut winter, with its freezing and thawing.

Once again, I called my friend Paul, a brawny, jovial property-maintenance guy at a nearby lake community. He had fixed the brakes and installed a muffler on our old jeep, and had painted its faded, worn body with leftover pea-green house paint! Paul's endless sense of humor, booming laugh, smiling face, sharp wit, and seeming ability to solve any problem made every task enjoyable. He had spent much of his life around farm equipment, and his very logical solution for installing several dozen posts three feet into the ground was to rent a post-hole digging machine. So he picked it up with his flatbed trailer and brought it to the vineyard one sunny morning. This unique little vehicle had a cockpit for the driver and a giant auger in the front measuring eighteen inches diameter! I placed a dot of orange spray paint exactly where we needed each post, twelve feet apart, and then Paul dropped the tip of its auger at the precise center of each hole location and drilled it downward into the ground, three and a half feet deep, spitting out boulders of glacial-till granite from almost every hole. The result was fifty-four post holes, each one taking about as much time to place as I spend polishing a pair of shoes—all in one morning. Bob and I placed posts in the holes, carefully leveling each one and then filling in, moving along behind Paul as he drilled more holes. The poles lined up nicely, contouring with the land. A terrific feeling of accomplishment followed the heavy labor of this landmark day. Now the field really looked like a vineyard, tops of the posts rolling up and down with the contours of the land, the soil below them tilled and ready to nurture our vines.

Our grapevines came as rootstock, with many tendrils streaming off of the main root. The central roots measured about a foot long, with side roots needing to be laid out circumferentially, a foot or so in each direction. To plant these properly, we needed 125 more holes measuring two feet in diameter and twenty inches deep. The auger we had used for the posts was not sufficiently wide and was gone anyway, so Bob and I dug these holes with shovels over the next few days, as the delivery of grape rootstock in early May was imminent.

In order to support the growing vines, we constructed a trellis. Shopping for trellis wire yielded some twelve-gauge wire on large spools from a local hardware store. Bob and I went to work, putting up three progressively higher wires to support our grapevines in their growth. These were stapled securely to each post and twisted at the ends. Only later did I find out that this technique was not ideal, so we revised the initial attachment to end posts with wire-tensioning devices drilled through the posts. This was fine at first, but by the third year these had been in place, they were rusted and frozen shut on the wires—so the wires might as well have been stapled!

But this didn't matter, as trellis wires were in place for our grape vines. We just needed to support the growing young vines so they could work their way up to the top wire. Long wooden stakes next to each new vine seemed to be a logical answer to support the initial vertical ascent to the first trellis wire.

Rootstock arrived in the sunny, warm second week of May 1999. Immediately after arrival, the young vines were gently extracted from their shipping boxes and soaked in buckets of water to prepare them for planting. Seeing these little vines in our garage preparing for a new lifelong home in our soil, next to our house, affirmed the transition about to occur in our lives, anticipating the fine grapes and wine that I knew these young vines would eventually yield.

FAMILY

S everal friends had expressed interest in planting grapes, but a few phone calls revealed that the only ones ready to pick up a shovel and watering can were my eighty-year-old father-in-law, Vincent John Brennan, and his wife (my mother-in-law) Martha. Lynn provided refreshments, encouragement, and photography documenting this momentous day in the early spring of 1999.

Grapevines intertwine in their connectedness, like family, and, in so doing, support each other, along trellising wires. These wires are necessary for the health and support of grapevines much as the fundamental support of family unity and its unconditional love are important for healthy human growth. Grapevines, with their twisty, unpredictable meanderings, lean toward light, as do those of us who are healthy in body and soul. Some move in ways that find lots of sun exposure and productivity, while other vines get lost in the tangle. Some crowd out others and cast shade over their fruit, such that disease might develop, so the grape grower's job is to cut back foliage sufficiently to allow enough light to keep all vines healthy, particularly trimming back the overly aggressive, "bull" vines as needed, so that a fair share of light is available to make each vine fruitful. The wayward vines must either be reoriented or cut.

I felt the sun strongly that misty May morning when my in-laws Vin and Marty arrived. They shared my vision and enthusiasm. We all cared and were excited about the future of these young grapevines in our family. We wanted to work together; we shared a healthy vision. The family bond was strong.

As we looked out through the mist toward the vineyard, ready to work, shovels in hand, it started raining. Nonetheless, we proceeded into the rain, which quickly subsided into a misting drizzle, to plant grapes. My father-in-law's quick sense of humor, which made light of the drizzle, set a perfect tone. After preparing the soil in each hole with composted manure, Vin or I would hold the chosen vine in its proper orientation and spread out the roots carefully, while the other placed enriched soil over and around the young roots. We kept each plant lined up with a stake that had been tied to the trellis wire above, to allow a stable configuration for the young vine to climb straight upward. My mother-in-law Martha followed along with a hose to water each newly planted vine. To encourage healthy and prompt growth, we placed a blue-tinted, tubular plastic sleeve around each plant, concentrating sunlight into a mini hothouse environment. These sleeves also gave further support to the young vines to help their vertical ascent. After a long, productive, wet, and happy morning, Lynn prepared a hearty soup for all of us. We dried off; sat back in the warm, dry comfort of our home; and watched the rain as it fell gently on our new vineyard.

HARMONY

A vineyard will not produce great grapes and ultimately fine wine with-out someone to prune, feed, nurture, and train its vines. Then comes the well-timed harvest and wine making, with methods best suited to each particular grape type. These human interventions, in order to be successful from year to year, must avoid injury to and disruption of the healthy processes working innately in the soil, environment, and grapes themselves.

Native grapes grow wild in some places. One might logically deduce that if he or she takes these naturally grown grapes and lets their juice ferment naturally, by the wild yeast that occurs in that place, a nice, natural wine will result. Wine has been, and still is, made this way. This spontaneous wine end product might be good with a truly unique character available only from the particular yeast of that place, or it could be a disaster. Natural yeast is risky.

The yeast sitting on grapes is unpredictable. The timing and conditions of a spontaneous fermentation are also arbitrary. To many experienced wine makers (particularly those trained through coursework reading, meeting at-tendance, and sharing ideas with others in the field), this approach (fully natural fermentation with local yeast) is rarely acceptable, given the many wonderful cultivated yeasts that can be matched in a custom way to specific grape types. In this way, one might expect to bring out the best qualities of each grape variety. This is not much different than matching food to wine. Some wineries, such as that of Dan Kravitz in the Languedoc-Rousillon region of southern France, routinely make wine with a natural yeast fermentation quite beautifully, such as his Chateau de Lancyre "Vieilles Vignes" 2007 Pic Saint Loup that I had an opportunity to taste at the Stowe, Vermont Grand Tasting in the summer of 2010. To have such cooperative local, spontaneously available yeast that will result in a wine of optimal character is surely a blessing, given the general unpredictability and vagaries of yeast. Such wines, however, are well worth pursuing, as recommended by Alice Feiring in her writings (5). Truly, the winery with a supply of grapes from a well-tended local environment is fortunate indeed. Some lucky vintners rely on a great working relationship between their grapes and the local yeast year after year. This is harmony at its best in a vineyard—mature grapes that come from a healthy environment, balanced by good sunlight, water, and sustainable soil; that produce abundant sugar and enough acid; and that then, with a bit of luck, are complimented by local yeast to produce a great (but not too fast) fermentation and a subsequent excellent, unique wine. The grape grower must simply be sure to cultivate and not injure in any way this somewhat intricate set of natural factors and interactions—which includes optimizing exposure to sun, opening the canopy, maximizing airflow, and controlling invaders without chemically damaging the place. In these ways, one may create a harmonious, sustainable environment for the best wine possible in that place and time. At times, I have thought of this as a model for how to live in the world—how many factors work into our daily lives and careers to produce a favorable and productive life experience.

While thinking about a healthy, productive environment, I was reminded of my stint working with a friendly, thoughtful, and considerate group of orthopedic surgeons on the governing board of the Arthroscopy Association of North America in 1990. The board president at that time had been very successful, not only as an orthopedic surgeon, but as a businessman, having started several companies from scratch. He promoted the idea of an Orthopedic Learning Center in which surgeons would study the intricacies of arthroscopic surgery by operating on cadaver knees and other joints instead of learning on live patients.

Her Knee

Her knee was
fluid precision,
Bavarian clockwork synchrony,
moving gracefully
through marathons and markets,
unconsciously loyal
until a wet rock
let go of her foot;
gravity prevailed,
and her knee struck
coastal granite.

There she lies, suspended by anesthesia,
fragments of bone and cartilage
sprinkled across the membranes of her knee—
crushed shards
where nature's complex creation
once surpassed any human design.

I was fortunate to serve on this board. Our president had an uncanny ability to create consensus, garner good will, and encourage enthusiasm, all with warmth, great planning, honesty, a sense of humor, and sincerity. He was uniquely capable, but more important than that was his consistent dedication, similar to the successful people described in Malcolm Gladwell's book *Outliers*. I believe that our board president was a Gladwellian outlier, because he did not just spend a little more time than others on the projects he chose, he worked tirelessly and put in far more effort than others. He knew how to instill harmony. He knew how to work cheerfully. The task of creating a major learning center never seemed to be overwhelming in his presence. In short, he was "a natural," much like a natural athlete who can excel by virtue of God-given talent.

One day he handed each of us a copy of "The Board Book," which pointed out that an effective board must be carefully constructed of individuals who can work harmoniously with each other. Even some of the more outspoken members of this board found respectful restraint in order to work with the group. This board laughed together frequently. Mutual respect was pervasive. The connectedness, interplay, and constructive attitudes of this board were no coincidence. Our president valued and cared about each member of the board, having participated in the selection of most; he assured a healthy balance of interests and individuals who would work together in the interest of greater good, in harmony. Some call this good "chemistry" or good "karma," but it is no coincidence. He was like a good vintner who assures sufficient sun, water, balanced soil, nutrients, and airflow for the vines in his (or her) care.

John Pryor Fulkerson

A Vineyard Villanelle

A grape is but a tiny ball
A world of pleasure it will bring
As summer lingers into fall.

Sweet blossoms near the bluebird's call
The bee and robin know it's spring
A grape is but a tiny ball

The day is full, the vines grow tall
A life of spirit, not of thing
As summer lingers into fall

Tending vines, blossoms small
Breezes gentle, bird on wing
A grape is but a tiny ball

Baskets full, the cart we haul
Preparing for the autumn fling
As summer lingers into fall

Joyful fellowship for all
With barrels full, our light hearts sing
A grape is but a tiny ball
As summer lingers into fall

Our New Vines

On awakening,
sunlight filtered through a curtain gap—
promising many splendid, ephemeral moments
in the light
of a new day

What a joy to see our little grape vines reaching for the first trellis wire! I stared down their grow tubes daily that first season—and yes, they were all climbing upward rapidly by the third week! We took the tubes off as the vines reached the first wire, to which they were then tied for support, as well as gently securing them to the wooden stake that had been placed next to each vine. The vines also helped hold themselves up with tiny tendrils thrown out like lassos to grab whatever they could find.

I set up Japanese beetle traps and walked around the vineyard each day after work, knocking the little invaders into a can half full of water and detergent. As July ended, the beetle population dropped off, and slightly cooler air swept in during that early August of summer 1999. With the major beetle invasion behind and traps full, a daily walk through the vineyard produced only fifteen to twenty Japanese beetles in August.

Nonetheless, vines had to be trained along the bottom wire, weeds removed, tilted stakes made vertical again, and unruly vine branches pruned. Time in the vineyard passes quickly.

Saturday, July 31, was sunny, hot, and clear at 9:15 a.m. Lynn's voice echoed from the back door: "John, get out of the vineyard; there's a bear!"

Strolling toward me, no more than fifteen or twenty feet away, was a lumbering, burly black bear. Spotting each other almost simultaneously, we both stopped and stood still for a few moments. The bear seemed surprised to see me, as I was to see him.

"Bear etiquette" was part of required training on a fishing trip to the Katmai Peninsula of Alaska earlier that summer. Our fishing guide said: "Don't stare at a bear. Walk away slowly, talk to the bear respectfully, don't turn your back on a bear, and try to look as big as you can, but don't be threatening."

In particular, I remembered one bit of advice: "Don't run away, because you will look like prey." So now, confronted with this bear in the vineyard, I didn't run, but I walked away, half backward, and quickly, as did the bear (diverting his path to move away from me). I watched this intruder out of the corner of my eye and noticed that he (or she) continued ambling along at a steady pace toward the woods. The bear didn't seem concerned about me, and I felt confident that he or she was more interested in eating our birdseed and blackberries than me.

Meanwhile, as I hustled through the back door, my son walked out and reminded me that black bears are berry eaters, so we both laughed about it as we watched the bear stumble slowly into the woods. It turned out that this bear was a coward anyway, as we later learned that our neighbor's cat had chased the bear up a tree in her backyard that same day!

Brad had rolled out of bed and looked out of his window to spot this husky black intruder wandering through our backyard that morning. Half asleep, his first inclination was that this was our black dog, Callie. It took only a second, however, for him to realize that this large animal was a bear, very close to the house. The bear had gone directly to each of our three bird feeders, and had knocked down two of them before standing on his hind legs to demolish the last. Surprisingly, he abandoned the last bird feeder, after bending down the post on which it was perched, when he heard Lynn's call to me in the vineyard. Apparently, he was frightened enough that he left much of the birdseed behind!

Such wandering creatures are silent neighbors, and we don't think about them much. They probably see us more than we see them. After a nearby sheep farmer shot a few coyotes, our local population of rabbits jumped precipitously the following summer. These rabbits could multiply more freely with fewer adversaries, and so the farmer's coyote killing allowed for an unusual propagation of rabbits that then feasted regularly on our vegetable garden. We had to place electric fencing around our garden and build a second inner fence, buried into the ground four inches (since rabbits like to burrow under wire fences) to preserve our lettuce, broccoli, and beans.

Our neighbor Mike and his cat went to the top of the vineyard one moonlit, starry evening—as he later described the event—and sat on an old bench up there, tipped back to watch the sky. After a short time, he heard deep snorting and grunting a short distance away, coming from the direction of the woods. The cat took off. What snorts in the New England woods? With ears and eyes wide open, Mike slowly rose from the bench and walked briskly and quietly. He said he felt hair standing up on the back of his neck as he walked down a vineyard row to the safety of his house. We all laughed when he told us this story the following day.

The Sacred Vineyard

Throughout history, sacred texts and self-help publications have proposed many formulas and courses of action in man's (and woman's) quest for meaning. The Hindu Bhagavad Gita, for example, advises one to "be free of attachment" to all things worldly, such that the human spirit might be released to engage directly with the source of all creation. To Hindus, that spiritual power, which might be known in other faiths as life force, God, Allah, or Yahweh, is the almighty source of all, as I understand it. This sense of a pervasive all-powerful force in the world may be similar to all believers, but defies adequate description in human terms. We can only hope to come into a better understanding of this power by being right-minded, loving, and sensitive to the beauty and order of the amazing natural world in which we live. "Our spiritual being is continually nourished by the countless energies of the perceptible world," according to the catholic theologian Pierre Teilhard de Chardin, in *The Divine Milieu*. Some come to know and understand this pervasive force, known as God to many, through prayer and meditation. The thirteenth-century Sufi mystic Rumi effectively addressed the Almighty in his poetry and writings:

> Today, like every other day, we wake up empty and frightened.
> Don't open the door to the study and pick up a book,
> Take down a musical instrument.
> Let the beauty we love be what we do.
> There are hundreds of ways to kneel and kiss the ground.
> The breeze at dawn has secrets to tell you.

Don't go back to sleep.
You must ask for what you really want.
Don't go back to sleep.
People are going back and forth across the doorsill
where the two worlds touch.
The door is round and open.
Don't go back to sleep.

Mystics access a connection with this mysterious and beloved source of all without doctrine. Buddhists, Taoists, and others use meditation and verse, haikus or poetry. "Let the beauty we love be what we do," says Rumi. Such beauty has the potential to put us in touch with the source of it all—God, if you will—at least for a while.

The great theologian Paul Tillich wrote of a "God above the God of theism," acknowledging an understanding of God as creator force beyond human definition, surpassing language and doctrine.

A vineyard embodies this power and harmony—creation emanating from the combined elements of soil, plant life, air, sun, water, and natural renewal. A type of garden, the vineyard requires human nurture in order to be at its best. This human engagement is natural and powerful. Enlightenment in a mighty creation becomes tangible. Much like love, in which we give ourselves over to another, putting their interest with ours and above ours, life in connection can carry one into caring and love beyond words. Communion comes to mind. Fortunate gardeners have this experience.

Others find this in sports; church; love; meditation; prayer; work; the creative process; or maybe when sitting or walking in or by an ocean, lake, field, woodland, mountain, stream, or river. Some find such enlightenment in the healthy human interactions of daily activities and also in travel. Travel brings this forth by opening doors to the broad expanse of our miraculous world.

The vineyard is another door to a realm beyond worldly concerns. Entering the vineyard, one may be fortunate to participate with it and its many components. Ego and worries fade into the background as one engages with it.

Cinque Terre

Sea foam bristling and rolling
below a hillside morning
in Monterosso.

Lemon-fresh anchovies, pesto, sea bream,
and vineyard-painted slopes
overlooking sunlit, azure swells
around the villas and shops of Corniglia.

Perfumed ribbons of air
weaving and rising
far above the strike and flow of Ligurian waters.

John Pryor Fulkerson

Morning Dew

Dew on the hay lot
above the pond at sunrise.
Condensed droplets
from fleeting cloud strokes
across the meadow last night,
spending this quiet dawn
near circles in the pond
where May flies emerge
from deep water.

Far, for the moment,
from mortality's call.
A sleepy aesthetic
and communion
beyond bread and wine
one crimson morning
in our vineyard.

Napa Valley

We traveled to California's Napa Valley in 1999, just as our new vines were prospering along their wires. Shoots, other than three or four at the level of each wire, had been removed from each of our vines. The plants looked healthy, and the Japanese beetles seemed to be under control. A careful scanning of the vineyard revealed three different little insects, but none matching those that my literature from Cornell indicted as criminals. Scattered powdery mildew was evident, so I gave the vines a dose of sulfur spray before we departed for the West Coast.

A stop in Seattle to lecture at the American Academy of Orthopedic Surgeons' "Summer Institute" led to dinner at the top of a tall building with a 270-degree view of Seattle and its surroundings. I was met there by the camaraderie of fellow orthopedic surgeons and a glass of Washington State chardonnay. I thought about this glass of chardonnay and how it, like the Hermitage wine we had opened upon returning from the Rhone River valley, evoked thoughts of fertile grape- and apple-growing expanses in the state of Washington. From the top of a building in downtown Seattle, I was transported to Washington State's lush hillsides and misty river valleys through the transformative magic of this wine working on my imagination. And the gentle nudge of the wine's alcohol eased the banter with new acquaintances at the reception, as the room brightened a bit with a deep sense of collegiality.

Two days later, Lynn and I met in San Francisco, rented a car, and drove off to Napa Valley wine country, with a stop in Sausalito to sample coffee served West Coast style. Sausalito had been an enchanting and funky little seaside village twenty to twenty-five years earlier, at the time of our previous visit there. At that time, there were steamy cafes and weathered doorways through which one could see the glistening bay. Now the town itself sparkled and boasted sleek, upscale shops. We ended up at Starbucks. The booming economy of the '90s had reworked this village to meet modern standards of comfort and affluence. The coffee was good, but I missed the old Sausalito.

Our Napa journey proceeded on a beautiful, sunny, warm day, when we encountered minimal traffic on our drive north. The Napa Valley abounded, as anticipated, in lush viticulture. At a small Oakville grocery store, we acquired fresh, "just out of the oven" bread; special cheese; cool green tea; and some interesting salads for lunch. Then we checked in at a little bed and breakfast in Calistoga. Our hostess provided a picnic table with umbrella in the garden, just off the living room, where we listened to a fountain nearby while discussing an afternoon bike route over our Oakville grocery picnic.

Riding bicycles allowed us to appreciate, up close, the abundant, verdant grape-laced tapestry surrounding and enveloping Calistoga and Napa. Local viticulture pervaded the community—vines were almost everywhere. Even the front yards of some smaller homes were neatly lined with productive vines instead of lawns. Different types of trellising; many grape types; old plants with thick trunks; and young, first-year vines proliferated all around. Many of the very old vines had never been trained properly, while many neat, young vines were held perfectly straight with two lateral shoots at the level of the lowest trellising wire. The predominant method was to strap down two lateral canes (new vines from the immediate past season), one right and one left, so that shoots would grow upward from each of these canes onto upper trellising wires. Some vines were trained along a higher wire. Training vines onto the trellis permits maximum exposure to airflow and sun. Plenty of sunlight is important for the formation of free volatile terpenes (FVTs) within grapes (FVTs are naturally occurring chemicals that give aroma and enhance the taste of wine).

We rode all around Calistoga and Napa on rented bicycles, noting pristine vineyard after vineyard. Toward the end of this first day's ride, we arrived at Chateau Montalena, a sensuous vineyard gem surrounded by pines and seemingly endless rows of grape vines. In a cool, faintly lit cellar tasting room, a few cheerful people stood at a long bar with wine glasses. An attractive young woman placed glasses in front of us on the bar, and we began our experience of Napa Valley wines.

"I think there's a hint of apricot?" a friendly woman offered regarding the wine that had just been poured, as she swished her glass around and inhaled thoughtfully with her nose perched on the edge of her glass. And indeed, a moment with the bouquet of this cabernet sauvignon revealed a faint, pleasant scent of apricot! This experience of tasting was new to us, so we spent a few minutes with each wine poured in our glasses and had fun detecting subtleties of taste and scent. After trying several Chateau Montalena wines, we bought a bottle of their cabernet sauvignon, placed it in the small backpack I was wearing, and rode slowly and happily back to our bed and breakfast.

We rambled to nine more wineries over the next few days in Napa and Calistoga, including Cakebread, Sterling, Grgich Hills, Raymond, Hess, and Opus, where we opted for a twenty-five-dollar taste of Opus I wine (1995). We thought this was very extravagant, but shared one taste, and spent lots of time studying the rich, complex scent and flavor of this special wine.

Another day, we went to the Russian River Valley Clos du Bois and Simi Vineyards. Lynn and I agreed that the Simi Sendal was the greatest taste experience of the journey. We bought a bottle to bring home with us, as one could carry wine onto a plane back in those days!

A Connecticut frost came and went quickly in early October. As I was heading out to work one brisk New England fall morning, a sea of tiny, frozen water crystals glistened all around. I approached my vines with trepidation. Those beautiful green leaves were stiffly erect in response to the sudden chill. "It's all part of the natural process," I told myself, but I was new to this, and the trauma to those healthy looking, full, broad leaves felt harsh—a stark warning of the bitter cold to follow. But I knew that the vines would be fine and that this was just the beginning of a winter's rest for them after a full summer in which they had gained strength to produce future grapes.

Two days later, when the sun was shining brightly, with temperatures in the sixties again, the severely wilted leaves were brown and pitiful. The first summer's growth had ended, so I began the process of pruning in preparation for the second season, which would coincide with the beginning of a new millennium and the twenty-first century.

The Mystery of Grapes and Wine

The unique effects of place and time on grapes and wine are mysterious. Many natural elements add value: the number of sunny, dry days which enhance the sugar and flavor of grapes; the soil; the care given to the grapes and vines; the water; the air; and everything in the wine-making process—from grape growth and crushing to yeast choices and quality of fermentation. Grapes are unique among fruits and widely acknowledged to produce wine superior to that from other fruit, partly, perhaps, because of their uncanny ability to capture some essence of the places from which they originate. The visceral response to a well-crafted wine is sensual. And, again, the root of this satisfaction, which changes with each different wine, is the mysterious connection of a wine with its place of origin.

When we think about vineyards, and the wines that flow from them, we might think about how they, like people, vary in quality and character. The healthy, positive sense we note in some people is not coincidental, any more than a well-tended vineyard or fine wine is coincidental or automatic. And, to be sure, imperfections create interesting challenges in people as they do in wines. Quirks might add "character" to people and to wine. Yet care and appreciation, when provided with love, work around quirks and help create beauty. From a male perspective, what makes a woman beautiful is, in many ways, the same as what makes a fine wine. When I think of an attractive woman, I think of all the details—her smile, her hair, her eyes, her speech, her grace, her personality, her intelligence, her integrity, her goodness, her contours, and how she moves. Of these qualities, integrity and goodness are most fundamental. I think about her presence and how her actions affect mine. I assimilate all the details, mostly unconsciously, as they blend together, such that a snapshot at that moment says "beauty." And these qualities will change from day to day and year to year. Aging tends to soften wine, as it does people. Thankfully, we all have different concepts of beauty in people, as we do of wine. As a wine "breathes" and "opens up," its true character and quality become increasingly evident, just as our sense of a person evolves as we allow his or her personality and nature to become evident. Perceptions vary greatly, though, and one person might consider raw milk distasteful, while someone else finds it sublime. What happens is (mostly) a subconscious synthesis of many qualities, which may, if so desired, lend itself to poetic understanding:

> When I see your beauty,
> All creation pauses
> In a vast moment
> Like the unified stillness
> After a train passes,
> Leaving one harmony

This unconscious, cumulative reaction to many subtleties is extraordinarily complex and different for each of us, given our unique experiences of life. Individual concepts of goodness and beauty may defy complete objective understanding. Shakespeare said, "The lover sees Helen's beauty in a brow of Egypt." Poetry helps, and is a powerful way to interpret concepts of goodness and beauty much as dreams fashion and interpret our deepest thoughts and concepts in ways that are usually incomprehensible.

So it is with people. So it is with marriage. When we've pulled the weeds, achieved good airflow, avoided toxins, and created a proper balance in the relationship canopy, we can fall in love again and again. One must become present to the person, as to the vineyard if it is to be good. One should choose grapes, as well as people, that are suited to one's environment, and then should nurture them. To produce a good wine, one must be devoted to the vineyard, free from distraction, completely present to the health of the vineyard and the wine making, and prepared to address problems as they arise. When one engages in a way that understands and is open to the beauty and integrity of the other, one becomes more complete as two worlds merge with deeper understanding and appreciation.

Wine and poetry are alike. When good, their complexities stir emotions and appreciation of the elements (soil or words, respectively) that create the experience. Through a merging of qualities, each component contributes to a unique integration, an appreciation that is not reproducible by any other means. This may be deeply felt at the core of one's being, much as it is for those fortunate enough to engage fully with great music. So we seek those that are to our liking, with a balance that appeals to us.

The trim, aesthetic vineyard contours; healthy green leaves; well-tilled, weed-free soil; openness; and airflow of the vineyard are essential to the balance, texture, tannins, aroma, color, taste, aftertaste, and light alcohol of the wine. And these blend with one's state of mind at a particular time to elicit a response. When one is fully engaged with a fine wine, particularly if one knows something about its origin, the experience of it will be optimal.

As stated earlier, wine captures some of the essence of the place where its grapes originate. And the same pertains to many natural products produced in different settings. If you want to know how good a particular tea or coffee is, make it with its pure leaves (tea) or beans (coffee), unflavored. Coffee growers and roasters will usually admit that they use their worst beans for flavored coffees. Sure, why not, if you are covering up the intrinsic flavor anyway! Aging in oak changes wine, just as flavoring coffee changes it. If a wine's flavor is one of oak, from the barrel in which the wine was aged, the purest essence of the wine and its place of origin are obscured, just as adding hazelnut to coffee covers the character of the original coffee beans. Both are fine—it's just a matter of what one is looking for.

Flavor and fragrance are the essence of good wine and are also very mysterious. These qualities are critically important in the food industry. Some people pay dearly for aged flavors and fragrances in wines. Vineyards succeed or fail depending on how well they deliver flavor and fragrance. As mentioned earlier, the native subtleties of wines are, in large part, brought to us by free volatile terpenes (FVTs) that produce scent and thereby much of the aesthetic experience of wine. FVTs become more abundant, most typically, in wines made from fully mature grapes. Their character may improve or deteriorate with time. They are responsible for the rich transformation of time and place that takes place upon experiencing a good wine. These floating molecules transport the essence of a wine and its origin into one's being. This journey is enriched by each subsequent taste of the wine.

A bold Tuscan sangiovese wine might evoke the rolling hills of central Italy, with its warm cultural commitment to great wine and food, in one who has been there or taken time to study the wine and culture of the region. When one knows the sangiovese grape, its wine might even evoke an awareness of Tuscan sun, its special soil, and generations of family tradition distilled through the years to produce beautiful wines in central Italy. Dolcetto or grappello grapes, grown in the same soil, will yield other unique wines with their distinct interpretations of origins. Wines produced from sangiovese, dolcetto, or grappello grapes grown in other places, such as California or Argentina, will have their own unique signatures, born in special soils and unique climates, using techniques refined by vintners of their own regions to optimize intrinsic qualities available from the grapes.

Brunello di Montalcino wine has been widely touted to be exceptional, and the brunello grape was believed to be unique to this region. Studies of brunello grapes of Montalcino, however, revealed that they are the same as sangiovese grapes. Yet the character of this wine is unique to the soil and environment of Montalcino.

With knowledge of a particular grape type and its place of origin, one may return to a beloved experience over and over. Having experienced sauvignon blanc in New Zealand and South Africa, I am transported to these places by their wines—I recall the rolling vineyards of Stellenbosch, South Africa, just beyond the surf of Cape Town, and feeling the warm sun there not too far from lions of the Kalahari Desert. Recently I was served a glass of sauvignon blanc from the Napa Valley in California and was captivated. It was so different from the sauvignon blancs of South Africa and New Zealand, yet it was clearly sauvignon blanc! The same sunlight that nurtures exquisite chardonnay grapes in the Napa Valley of California had produced rich sauvignon blanc that was more "full bodied" than the light grapefruit and steel of its New Zealand relatives or the lemony sauvignon blanc we loved in South Africa. The journey was different, and we happily defined what we liked. Some prefer the sauvignon blanc of California, just as some like Starbucks coffee while others prefer cold brew from Trader Joe's.

2000

We were concerned about our vineyard the following winter, particularly when temperatures dropped far below zero degrees Fahrenheit. There had been little snow that first winter and therefore no protection for the vines (snow, ironically, insulates grafted vines and their roots from bitter, freezing winds and harshly frigid temperature shifts). Fortunately, during the fall, my daughter had helped me heap up soil around the vines, where *vinifera* had been grafted onto hardy rootstock, affording added protection of this critical part of each plant. Only time would tell what kind of attrition would occur. There was no reason to think any more about it until April.

In April, though, it was time to cut back damaged vines. Pruning shears in hand, I cut off old vines until only green, live wood was left. This didn't leave much, but it was clear that certain varieties were doing better. The chardonnay and riesling flourished, or so it seemed. The cabernet and gewürztraminer, however, had been damaged by the arctic, winter wind that year. Dead wood harbors disease, so I removed it completely, leaving only healthy vines. Further complicating the winter damage was residual black rot, so I looked into a more potent treatment to prevent a surge of this pesky invader in the warmth of summer. Although the sulfur sprays of the previous seasons had kept down powdery mildew, these were ineffective against black rot, and therefore it was necessary to add something else. I had been naive in my effort to minimize sprays and realized that it was now time to deal with the known problems in our vineyard. Black rot had done some damage the previous year, and I was going to eradicate it, if possible.

The young vines' growth proceeded slowly that second season, and cabernet lagged the most. The lowest part of our small vineyard, where cold air accumulated during the winter months, yielded less vigorous growth. Even a few degrees' temperature difference affected the vigor of the vines.

Meanwhile, my hybrid daylilies, inspired by Uncle Currier, were in their second season and produced blossoms just as little clusters of grapes were forming on our vines. The daylily parents had been selected to create a specific cross by applying pollen from one daylily parent's anther (those big stalks with pollen-laden pods on the ends) to the pistil (the pointy female receptor, toward the center of a flower) of the other carefully selected parent. The recipient mother's blossom was tied in order to keep it hidden from a bee that might bring unwanted pollen to its pistil. The resulting seedpod would contain seeds of the specific cross. I had harvested hybrid seeds two years previously, kept them in our refrigerator that winter, and planted them the following spring. The lily offspring, like people, were all unique, and I decided to name the first three varieties after my wife and children.

The summer of 2000 was wet! The vines' growth was pitiful compared to that of the previous sunny, dry summer of 1999. A few sprays for black rot and mildew helped. Nonetheless, it was so wet that these blights still took a toll because of my inadequate preventive measures of the previous year. Consultation with a local commercial vintner revealed that persistent spraying, every other week or more, would be necessary to prevent irreparable damage from mildew and rot.

Roving deer that summer knocked back the injured plants even more, nibbling off some of the burgeoning new-vine growth. Japanese beetles also took some foliage, and the plants looked sad compared to the bountiful growth and leaf production of 1999. We hoped for abundant growth in 2001, when the plants would be more mature with heartier roots.

One highlight of the 2000 season was an opportunity to make wine with neighbors—an ear, nose, and throat surgeon and his wife, their young family, and their friends. Frank had purchased five hundred pounds of California cabernet sauvignon and was set up to crush, press, and ferment the sweet grape juice in his basement.

The grapes arrived at Frank's home on a brilliant, colorful, late-September day. The grapes were deep red, sweet, and lush from a long California growing season. Family and friends gathered, as the kids loaded grapes into a traditional-Italian hand-crank grape crusher. Everyone took a few turns at the crusher. All of the juice and skins went into a large vat, which was placed in a cool place. Yeast and sulfite were added later, and the grape must (juice to be fermented into wine) was covered to keep out flies attracted by the sweet juice. The aroma of this juice permeated the room as a bottle of last year's wine was opened for the celebratory libation and feast, which started with cheese- and meat-stuffed cherry peppers; mozzarella cheese in virgin olive oil; and fresh, crusty bread. We were all elated about the forthcoming fermentation.

The following week's pressing, in an old-fashioned wine press, of the wine skins (which had fermented along with the juice to add color and flavor to the wine) brought our families together again under Frank's enthusiastic leadership. Every available luscious drop of the new wine was extracted from the skins that had been pressed to a hard, round cake of compacted wine skins. We poured the fragrant new wine into five-gallon glass carboys for aging. Then the carboys were sealed from oxygen by twisty, little air locks that allowed bubbles of carbon dioxide (from residual fermentation) to leave the container, while blocking air, specifically oxygen, from entering (if air gets to the wine, it will spoil, turning it into vinegar under the influence of oxygen-requiring

Acetobacter bacteria). Oh, how sweet the air smelled with the newly fermented wine!

As glasses of the new wine were passed around generously, the air was full of laughter. Frank brought out bottles of his previous vintage for comparison. Pizza from the outdoor wood-fired brick oven, antipastos, and special casseroles appeared. The crushing and pressing of grapes had been intoxicating. The food and wine made us one for that time.

2001

The new buds were plump and healthy in May 2001. Unfortunately, on May 27, 2001, a killing frost settled in after the temperature dropped precipitously to twenty-eight degrees Fahrenheit that previous night. Virtually all the initial growth was killed, but some of the healthier plants, most notably riesling, bounded back from some surviving buds, but the cabernet franc, gewürztraminer, and chardonnay suffered. In their second year, the Marechal Foch vines grew very well, proving their cold-hardiness, and provided a small harvest of grapes at the end of the growing season.

Foch was named after the famous World War I French army general, Ferdinand Foch, supreme commander of the Allied forces in World War I that ultimately defeated the Germans, yielding a peace accord at the Treaty of Versailles. In honor of this powerful commander, Eugene Kuhlman created the Marechal Foch grape in Alsace. This hybrid of goldriesling and Oberlin noir (a gamay–*Vitis riparia* hybrid originally from Burgundy, France) is cold hardy and relatively easy to grow in Connecticut.

Spraying for mildew and black rot every ten days to two weeks had protected the harvest and prevented any resistant mildews from developing.

It was a fairly dry year, but the growth of the vines was disappointing. Was it the previous year's black rot? Or maybe it was the killing frost of May? I found the most likely answer the following spring at the annual Connecticut Wine Course, when I spoke with the vintner and viticulturist from Chamard vineyard, who thought the disappointing growth was most likely a problem of inadequate nutrition, not infection. We had lost vines, probably a third of the cabernet and chardonnay. Although I had tried to net the grapes adequately, one afternoon a flock of starlings consumed our small six-cluster yield of Foch!

Yet at the end of the season, there was some riesling that had survived behind netting. One thrilling experience was crushing two clusters of riesling, providing just enough juice to fill a small glass. It was oh so sweet a reminder of what would be possible! We shared and savored every drop of our year's production!

Determined to make wine, we purchased chardonnay grape juice and, with the help of several books, got a fermentation going with Montrachet yeast added to the store-bought juice that I had placed in a large sterilized bucket. This produced a dry, flower-scented white wine, which we poured into a sterilized, air-locked, five-gallon glass carboy to mature. A few months later, we transferred the wine into recycled, thoroughly cleansed wine bottles. This effort yielded twenty-six bottles of surprisingly tasty chardonnay with a slight scent of lavender—another highlight of our 2001 season.

2002

Foch vines flourished in the spring of 2002. We planted some additional hardy hybrids, Cayuga and Vidal blanc, to replace the lost *vinifera*.
Cayuga, named for the magnificent Lake Cayuga of Cornell University (far
above Cayuga's waters) fame, was created at the New York State Agriculture
Experiment Station in Geneva, New York to be durable in cold weather and
excellent for making wine.   Grape hybridizer Jean Louis Vidal created Vidal
blanc to make cognac, but the grape found its real calling as a good grape for
white wine, particularly ice wine, and had grown well in the cold climates of
Ontario, Canada, the New York Finger Lakes region and northern Sweden,
not far from the arctic circle! These locations made Connecticut seem tropical
by comparison.   However, it would be at least two years from the planting of
these special vines until we would have a chance to taste their grapes.

Meanwhile, summer 2002 brought a bumper crop of blackberries. A small
family reunion with my wife's aunts and uncles ended with an afternoon of
energetic berry picking. Some who weren't picking blackberries were driving
golf balls over or into the pond behind our house. Some made plans to create
blackberry jam or blackberry pie. The volume of blackberries was such that
everyone took home a few quarts, leaving some of the harvest for Lynn and
myself. The result, for us, was thirteen pounds of wild blackberries.

Having never made fruit wine or even wine from grapes, I looked up recipes in Gene Spaziani's book on making wine(6). Two other recipes for blackberry wine—one from a newspaper and one from a book were helpful also.

I crushed the berries on a Saturday, adding some water, as recommended, and then sugar to bring the brix (percent sugar) to 22, appropriate for a fermentation to wine. The juice then sat overnight on top of the crushed berries. The following day was Sunday, and I had naively overlooked the need for yeast and pectic enzyme (to release juice from the crushed berries) that afternoon. My wine-making supply store was closed, so I went to a nearby vineyard and found the wine maker. This elderly, neatly dressed Italian gentleman took time to talk with me while John Phillip Sousa music played in the background, where their staff was busily finishing a day's work that Sunday. He provided not only some Montrachet yeast, but also yeast nutrient to stimulate the fermentation.

Upon returning home, I immediately started the yeast fermenting in a cup of warm water, sugar, and nutrient and then added this fermenting yeast to the sweet blackberry juice that was sitting on top of all the crushed berries, which would enhance the color and character of the wine.

The fermentation proceeded steadily, and within a week we tasted our first blackberry wine. It spilled out a fragrance of complex fruit. Not just blackberries, but some licorice too, wafted by when we sniffed and tasted the new wine—how pleasant to experience such a fragrance emanating from fermented wild blackberries! This, then, became a dry, tart blackberry wine—something quite distinct from the original blackberry juice, miraculously transformed by fermentation. In retrospect, it might have tasted even better if I had added a bit of sugar (back-sweetening) to the final product, but it was a good, dry wine and went into glass jugs with air locks to undergo a secondary malolactic fermentation to soften it while all the little berry fragments and spent yeast dropped away to the bottom of the jugs. We let it sit for two months until it cleared enough for racking (siphoning the wine off of the old, spent yeast) and eventual bottling.

Another great thrill of 2002 was the riesling and gewürztraminer harvest. Lynn and I picked the remarkably small yield of grapes in less than twenty minutes! It was only a few salad bowls full of grapes but was, nonetheless, a harvest of our own grapes. These grapes had a light lime-green hue with a peachy luster that seemed to glimmer slightly as the soft autumn sun played on them where they sat in four large salad bowls by our vineyard. The supremely fresh grapes glistened as we sorted and washed them. It took about ten minutes to compress the rich, thick juice from these grapes. This combined riesling and gewürztraminer grape juice was opaque with grape pulp and specks of crushed seeds distributed through the lush, fragrant, sweet, fresh juice. Its brix was 19 and required some dilution of acid by adding water. Sugar was added to a brix of 22, suitable for the fermentation, and the juice was transferred to a large bucket in which fermentation would take place.

Starting the fermentation was not easy. Forty-eight hours passed after I added yeast, and nothing happened. Warming the must (juice) was said to help, so I carried the fermentation container to our upstairs bathtub and filled the tub with warm water around the precious bucket of juice. The tub had to be replenished with warm water every few hours to keep it warm enough to make a difference. After another day of watching and praying, the fermentation finally started.

This fermentation then buzzed along steadily, and in a few days, we found a perfectly dry Connecticut riesling, which I transferred to sterilized-glass cider jugs with air locks.

As the vineyard shut down that fall of 2002, the new riesling wine sent a sweet scent around the counters and wine racks of our newly improvised wine cellar. Tartrate crystals precipitated on the inner surfaces of the glass jugs, reducing the acidity of this young wine. I marveled at how the wine regulated itself to be more optimal—softer and less acid as it dispensed of crystalline tartaric acid onto the jug walls. I bottled this wine in December after the yeast had settled enough (I thought).

By February, having moved on to other activities and not thinking much about the wine for several weeks, I went down into the cellar to see how it was doing and found that two corks had shot out! These precious bottles of riesling had continued fermenting (thereby forming carbon dioxide) in the corked bottles—because there was too much sugar and yeast in wine that I had bottled too early. The residual yeast then restarted a fermentation of the remaining sugar, forming carbon dioxide in the corked bottles—ultimately creating enough pressure to drive out a couple of corks. This process, leaving a little yeast in the bottle to produce carbon dioxide, is the same as that used in making champagne (which is why they wire down the corks of champagne bottles).

I took a bottle up to the kitchen and uncorked it. Violently foaming wine shot out onto the floor and onto my shirt! Ten bottles of riesling champagne, without reinforced corks, remained. In order to have some bottles for future use, I decided we would open (cautiously) two bottles that showed evidence of partial cork extrusion and would save the rest, hoping that the corks would hold (their corks looked secure, with no protrusion at that time)! The wine was good, and improved from the previous fall. The spritz of this riesling champagne was really refreshing, with a slight peach taste, softened by secondary fermentation and tartaric-acid crystallization. It was *our own* riesling, and we cherished and savored it. We shared it with friends. But we also lost two more bottles, so by April we had consumed all the remaining riesling before natural carbon-dioxide production sent any more of this precious wine onto our cellar floor!

The energy and time spent to produce that riesling were immeasurable, and so too were the depth of experience and pleasure of sampling and sharing *our* wine. Drinking the wine brought back how it had come to be—even the gentle warmth of that late-summer harvest day, along with the smiles, the laughs, and the joy we felt as we harvested a few clusters of grapes in our backyard vineyard. This first full process of making wine had been successful enough. The soil adjustment, grapevine planting, pruning and care of the vines, picking, crushing, pressing, fermentation, and bottling had yielded a riesling wine unique to our "terroir."

Integrity

I was just here—
a myriad of intervening moments since then—
countless interwoven elements
ebbing and mingling,
mysteriously taut with purpose,
the unique tapestry of these encounters
providing enrichment to the cellular level.
Each country walk distills
such immersions
into precious memory.

One of the great surprises and pleasures of growing grapes and making wine is joining forces with the marvelously balanced, wondrous natural world. When problems occur, nature always manages to restore balance, not necessarily in ways that are advantageous to certain plants or animals (including us human beings), but balance nonetheless. Tectonic plates shift and earthly pressures erupt, causing earthquakes and tsunamis, while tornadoes and hurricanes disrupt our human ways, but eventually balance returns. So it is with biological systems. Take our bodies, for example: appropriate production and modulation of hormones, persistent cardiac function, nerve transmission, thought, vision, and so on. We expect these miracles, but they rely on sensitive, balanced, self-regulating processes. All those little cells work away purposefully without our awareness and without any human intervention necessary to do their complex jobs. Doctors intervene when disease occurs, with medications and surgery, and modify paths of cellular function with diet and care of our bodies and minds, but the machinery of all those complex cells is extraordinarily capable and independent, usually restoring and healing with little or no help.

At their best, cellular functions are integrated. Cells and molecules work together in coordinated ways, until something goes drastically wrong, like cancer. Then we have to remove the disease with surgery or find other ways to disrupt it. Cancer occurs when cells no longer cooperate and work together. Cancerous cells spin off and do as they please, moving to parts of the body where they don't belong, growing there inexorably to cause problems and eventually to destroy otherwise integrated, functional processes.

Like a healthy body, grape vines interact in highly coordinated ways when they are free of disease, supplied with sufficient sunlight and water, and growing in good soil with healthy microorganisms and nutrition in proper balance. When all the elements balance, the vineyard is harmonious. But without proper tending, grapevines will go wild, producing little fruit, as uncontrolled weeds use important soil nutrients and crowd the vines, blocking sun and harboring dampness that mildew, black rot, and other diseases love.

John Pryor Fulkerson

A vineyard works well as a metaphor for human living. Its tortuous, unpredictable growth requires some trimming, guidance, and nurturing. Just as we prune away excessive and destructive vines in a successful vineyard, we must remove unnecessary and destructive behaviors that consume our precious time. Pruning allows better access to light and air. Excising all the extraneous, cumbersome, superficial outer growth promotes good fruit by channeling sun toward the grapes. When a fresh breeze flows easily into the open canopies of our lives, indifference, meanness, judgment, overindulgence, laziness, crudeness, and other poisonous behaviors are swept away. The light of hope that nourishes good values encourages healthy fruit and ultimately a balance of love, mutual respect, and companionship. None of this is completely spontaneous. Attention to details makes all the difference.

2003

Winter 2003 brought severe cold and an abundance of snow. White, billowing mounds of it folded around our diminutive bare vines, which poked their naked vulnerability out into the air and sun. I pruned carefully and hoped that fruit would appear in 2003, hopefully with an early boost from an abundant watering of melted snow.

The snowmelt was further enhanced by heavy rain that spring. All this water softened the sweet-smelling, early, green grass. The sun hardly appeared before June, but neither did any frost, so buds swelled and grapevines blossomed abundantly. Marechal Foch grew quickly, but the sparse remaining *vinifera* (chardonnay, cabernet, and gewürztraminer in particular) had receded from the stark winter cold. Even the riesling, which had done fairly well the previous season, was sluggish. In fact, some of it perished, as did most of the chardonnay and cabernet. We had thought the snow cover would protect our grafted vines, but this did not happen. Maybe it was just too cold for *vinifera* in the Litchfield hills.

Fortunately, we had planted Foch, Cayuga, and Vidal blanc the previous year, to replace *vinifera* lost in the winter of 2002. As hoped, they thrived. The older Foch boasted many blossoms and later many, many clusters of grapes. The native Cayuga vines, in their second year, grew steadily, particularly after a generous application of aged manure, along with a sprinkling of balanced fertilizer and plenty of rain. The riesling, our most cherished *vinifera*, never regained its vigor.

In late June, some of the tender new-vine growth had been mysteriously clipped and left dangling. A quick review of information obtained on the internet introduced a likely culprit—the grape-cane girdler, a two-millimeter black beetle that amputates the tips of new vines and drops a few eggs in the remaining damaged vine, from which larvae emerge the following season to clip more new vines and start the cycle again. By walking through the vineyard every other day, I spotted and captured a few of these nasty little beetles and excised the damaged growth, along with the egg cases that had presumably been deposited there. The alternative to pesticide was frequent walks through the vineyard, an overall pleasant chore. I carried pruning shears in one hand, and in the other, a basket to collect and then dispose of damaged growth containing a next generation of grape-cane girdlers. By mid-July I had eliminated the girdlers—which was very satisfying—without using pesticide. I was beginning to understand sustainable agriculture.

The summer was wet, like the spring had been, and cool. None of the vines flourished except Foch, which grew exuberantly, producing a generous yield of small, dark-purple, almost black grapes. At times, powdery mildew appeared in a few small sections of the vineyard. Because of the dampness-related disease the previous year, considerable medicine (sulfur) and surgery (removal of diseased grapes and vines) were necessary to maintain the vineyard's health.

SURGERY

I learned a lot about life and disease during two years as a general medical officer and surgeon at the Fort Defiance Native American Hospital in New Mexico. The Navaho people form cholesterol "gallstones" in their gallbladders instead of coating the inner walls of blood vessels with deadly cholesterol plaque. In this way, they stay remarkably free of coronary artery disease and heart attacks, but are very vulnerable to gallbladder congestion and infection (cholecystitis) when little stones drop into and plug the gallbladder's cystic duct. Fat in the diet promotes gallbladder attacks, so we saw plenty of gallbladder trouble in this population of fascinating, beautiful people who love their lamb and fried bread.

Removing sick gallbladders was routine at our hospital on the Navaho reservation where I was stationed for two years after completing surgical-internship training. In those days, before endoscopic surgery, gallbladder removal required a six-inch (or more) incision under the ribs (the "costal margin"). The muscles were split and retracted as necessary, and the protruding sick gallbladder was easily identified under the liver. Dissecting it free, in most cases, was pretty easy—a couple of secure ties placed around the cystic duct of the gallbladder, one cut between them, and the diseased organ was sent to the pathology lab (all of this can be done with a scope and three or four little incisions these days). Occasionally there might be a wayward gallstone to be tracked down and removed from a blocked common bile duct. This routine was usually uncomplicated, requiring the patient to stay for a short while in our hospital before going home sore but grateful, feeling better with the sick organ removed and overall health restored.

The first female Navaho surgeon, Dr. Lori Arviso Alvord, describes how she brought the healing powers of native American spirituality to the operating room in her book entitled *The Scalpel and the Silver Bear(7)*. She points out that the spirit brought by a surgeon to an operating room affects the patient and the eventual outcome. Says Dr. Lori Arviso Alvord: "Although a surgical procedure focuses on a single organ, I always tried to stay aware of the whole person- organs, mind and spirit, the harmony of their entire being."

One of our patients had suffered with gallbladder disease for several years without treatment. He was really sick, with a high fever and excruciating pain under his ribs that penetrated back to his shoulder blade. This gentle Navaho man had developed a chronic gallbladder infection with little response to several days of antibiotics. The senior general surgeon decided to remove his ailing gallbladder. I was the assistant surgeon, fresh out of surgical internship and I saw that an important part of my role was to care for the whole patient, with sensitivity to him, his culture and his suffering. He trusted us because we considered everything about him, not just his gallbladder.

We brought this ailing, feverish Navaho patient to the operating room, where he was given general anesthesia, a thorough prep of his belly with antiseptic soap, and then a generous incision to ensure adequate exposure of the very diseased biliary tract. My young surgical eyes had never seen such a sick, deformed gallbladder. The senior surgeon was quiet and wary. Distention showed where the gallbladder was located in a bed of inflamed, swollen, adherent scar tissue. An edge was dissected to free up this gallbladder from the adjacent liver. This sick, bulging area, however, was highly distorted, and so the surgical dissection produced a leak from the liver itself, which could not be clearly differentiated as separate from the gallbladder through the poorly defined scar tissue. The patient finally recovered after intensive treatment with drainage, antibiotics, and careful attention to details at every step. During his recovery, he required three different antibiotics to treat recurrent resistant infections after the initial bacteria had been defeated. We got to know him very well through his ordeal and learned that he wished to engage the help of his family spiritual healer- a Navaho medicine man. The healing process was enhanced by the chanting, singing, and presence of the medicine man who came to our ward each afternoon along with family members and friends. This brought a great sense of hope, stability, good will and confidence which surely helped our patient. Our patient recovered steadily from his difficult and complicated disease. I still believe the medicine man helped. Most surgeons have a sense of which patients will do best after surgery, largely based on positive or negative attitudes, confidence, and trust. When we treat the whole person and his or her surrounding environment, not just the local infestation, a favorable outcome is more likely.

Prevention, accurate diagnosis, comprehensive treatment of all contributing factors, and surgery (pruning away the sick parts), when necessary, are part of vineyard care as they are in surgery.

Despite adequate preparation and spraying, a damp, warm season can activate spores of powdery mildew, downy mildew, black rot, phomopsis cane rot, and other pesky infestations, particularly when the days are warm and steamy—thus creating a perfect incubator for disease in the vineyard. Fortunately, one can eliminate, or at least contain, disease once it is identified. Usually, careful spraying and removal of damaged foliage and berries will banish the unwelcome invaders, but spores hang around and can become resistant, just like human infections. Given too much time for mildew and black rot to penetrate the vineyard, plants and even a whole crop can be lost. The grape grower must maintain a clean, healthy balance in the entire vineyard after removing disease, allowing good air flow, sun and nutrients to avoid recurrence.

HARVEST 2003

In August, we biked all around the Champlain Islands of nearby rural Vermont, stopping for swims or tastes of local fare whenever we found a general store or diner. We discovered an enchanting vineyard with attached winery very near Lake Champlain. The owners and staff there were friendly and enthusiastic to share their experience, particularly when we talked of growing grapes and making wine in Connecticut. This vineyard was nurtured by warm air from Lake Champlain during colder times of the year, enabling it to survive its northern Vermont location and making viticulture feasible in a sometimes-frigid part of northern New England. Such large bodies of water hold onto some heat with their thermal mass and then emit it back when temperatures drop. In mid-August, plenty of maturing clusters seemed to be flourishing in this lovely, windswept lakeside vineyard, so a good harvest seemed likely, barring mildew or black rot infestation, early frost or massive bird attacks. They were growing Baco noir, as well as Foch and Cayuga. We sampled their wines and relished their unique flavors. By using the right grapes for their locale and then sound winemaking techniques, they were producing rich, flavorful wines from grapes grown in northern New England. We decided to add Baco noir, created by Francois Baco, to our vineyard.

Meanwhile, birds had been feasting on our pending harvest during this time away, so I acquired fourteen-foot-wide bird netting as soon as we arrived back in Connecticut. With the help of my neighbor Kevin, we covered the grapes with nets by installing net supports from pole to pole, thus creating a long, tent-like structure of broad netting over our grapes to protect them from birds. Despite this, an occasional starling or sparrow would find a loose-netting access point and squeeze in for some fresh grapes. Getting these birds out was a challenge. They were essentially caged in with the vines and didn't seem to remember how they got in or how to get out. Typically, I would lift up one side of the netting and then chase the bird(s) out by running up and down the other side waving my arms. This would take a while, as the bird would fly back and forth past the opening I created until finally, usually by chance, it seemed, the bird would frantically dart out of the temporary exit. These occasional birds did little damage.

By mid-September, Foch was prolific and healthy. I went around testing the sugar levels of grapes from different parts of the vineyard with my hand-held spectrophotometer. The device has a clear, flat surface onto which to squeeze a couple drops of grape juice in order to determine a sugar level. After one places the finger-crushed grape juice on this surface, a little door closes onto the juice to spread it out so that one can hold it up to light and take a direct spectrophotometric reading of the sugar in a grape. The brix was 16 on average after testing many grapes and some combined juice. The brix needed to hit 18-20 to optimize the wine flavor and acidity. As the days were getting shorter and the nights cooler, the possibility of frost loomed. A frost would freeze our grapes' thin skins and cause them to burst on the vine if we waited too long to harvest. We decided to invite some friends to join our harvest the following week, hoping that the brix would rise a little more before then.

Picking Grapes Before Breakfast

I dreamed that I was picking grapes before breakfast.
After clipping the first few clusters,
the smell of fresh coffee
was wafting around
near whole-wheat toast and Lynn's blackberry jam,
but that would wait,
because I was already picking grapes,
humming as the buckets filled,
marveling at the taut grape clusters
and their abundant sweet ripeness
that would run from our wine press,
surrounded by friends and family
at the end of the day's harvest.

Our friends and family gathered. Stuart (a wine-collecting friend) and I peeled back netting, and Foch-picking began! Some decided to sort grapes, picking out the green, immature ones, while the rest of us picked and washed the newly harvested grapes. After about two hours, we were ready to crush, so we took all the sorted Foch grapes into our winemaking room. Ten-year-old Sarah wanted to put her feet in the grapes to stomp on them, Lucille Ball–style, but we were able to persuade her to turn the crank on the crusher instead. Our son, Brad, encouraged everyone, Tom Sawyer style, to turn the long handle of the crusher. The result was about ten gallons of rich-looking, deep-purple grape juice with all the stems and skins mixed in. That night, Brad and I added some water to soften the juice acidity, which was pretty high as expected from our early harvest after a short, wet growing season. We chilled the juice (the must) with a couple of sealed, ice-filled containers that I had prepared for this purpose. The next day, we added Pasteur red yeast to the juice, skins, and remaining stems to start the long-awaited fermentation.

My friend Eric and his wife, Candace, stopped by the following Saturday, just when the juice was ready for pressing. In a small wooden wine press donated by a friend (who used to make wine), we pressed the lush skins in order to extract as much additional wine as possible, keeping the free run (unpressed) wine separate. Afterward, we placed the new wine in five-gallon carboys with air locks, and I tossed a few French oak chips in to impart a bit of oak character to our batch of new Foch wine.

After the carboys of new wine were tucked away on the cool floor of our basement, Lynn and I went to a nearby commercial vineyard's fall-harvest party and spent a lazy late afternoon with some friends, listening to music and sipping the vineyard's previous-season wines. One highlight was an eiswein (sweet dessert wine made from very late-harvest grapes with very high sugar), made from Connecticut Vidal blanc grapes. By late afternoon, as autumn shadows highlighted the early-fall New England brilliant foliage colors, the sun was still warm, and fiddle music filled the air. Our harvest had been successful, and our wine was secure. We were immersed in the wine of north-west Connecticut as our 2003 grape-growing season came to a close.

The winter that followed was exceptionally cold. Temperatures dropped below negative fifteen degrees Fahrenheit one night, and one spell of brutally cold weather lasted several days. Fortunately, Our cold weather hardy hybrids were able to withstand very harsh weather and temperatures as low as negative forty degrees Fahrenheit. Durable and resistant to disease, our hybrid vines were all right after the rigors of a bitter northwest Connecticut winter.

Mortality

Tempered steel touches the soul
At times
Clouds move unpredictably
in many ways.
They can't be thrown aside
like a down comforter.
Mortality peels the outer core
patiently

Cold-Weather Grapes

Elmer Swenson was born and raised in Osceola, Wisconsin, where the growing season is short, like that in the hills of northwest Connecticut. He inherited his grandfather's farm and wanted to grow good grapes for making high-quality wine despite the relatively short summers and cold winters of Wisconsin. At the age of thirty, he began hybridizing grapes, crossing French hybrid grapes with *Vitis riparia*, local grapes that thrive in cold weather but make mediocre wine. Through this painstaking process, Elmer produced a few wonderful varieties, among them Saint Croix, that make excellent wine like their European ancestors yet endure very cold temperatures like their domestic parent, *Vitis riparia*. Elmer shared his grape cuttings generously and patented several of his brilliant hybrids, which made possible the growing of fine grapes in cooler climates such as those of Wisconsin and Connecticut. Elmer was not alone, as other hybridizers around the world also were creating cold-hardy grape hybrids.

I felt very fortunate to have grapes suited to our climate, and some of the new hybrids were producing terrific wines that I had opportunities to try at gatherings of the Connecticut Vineyard and Winery Association. These grapevines were tough, and I prayed that they could endure the cold so that we would have good harvests for years to come. I had been talking to fellow vintners and grape growers in Connecticut, who had lost *vinifera* in previous years, and they were well pleased with the durability and resilience of their French-American hybrid grape vines.

TASTE

Vegemite is a curious salty paste, loved in Australia, but less appreciated by those who are not used to it. Likewise, some connoisseurs pay dearly to savor Beluga caviar (fish eggs), which repels many of those who first encounter this "gourmet" appetizer. Certain liquors have special appeal to those who, by virtue of culture, opportunity, or chance, learn early of their special qualities and characters. Scotch and cognac come to mind. Long aging adds even more to the experience, as chemical processes soften harsher qualities while accenting more-desirable aspects of the spirit. These are just a few examples of tastes that some love and others shun. Sometimes, we come to believe that high-cost delicacies are "better," even if our palate says otherwise.

For example, while traveling in Spain, Lynn and I were invited to have lunch with the owner of a large vineyard not far from Portugal. The delicacy that day was eel, much loved in that region. While Lynn and I respected and appreciated the local tradition and palate, consuming a portion of the eel was a little difficult for us. We did not have a "taste" for it.

When one grows to appreciate a flavor, learning perhaps from others that a particular taste is superior to other tastes, his or her mind often accepts the doctrine. Many of us have to learn about certain tastes, and then work at them, before we are able to accept them as "good." Anyone for some raw milk, Vegemite, eel, or caviar?

Some of the newer grape varieties offer wonderful and unique wine characters when tended well and then fashioned into good wine. First tastes of new varietals, when compared to established wines, can be confusing. Where is the traditional flavor of wine? But with patience and appreciation of the new experience, one might develop a "taste" for it. Depending on the grape type and the care taken in preparing the wine, one might enjoy the new experience and perhaps even seek out the newly acquired taste.

Well-made cabernet sauvignon is a hard-to-beat red wine, yet a good red zinfandel, pinot noir, or petit syrah is just right sometimes. The list of alternatives will grow as time passes, winemaking knowledge grows, new varietals become more widely available, and wine lovers seek unique experiences in wine. Some individuals will surely prefer a nice glass of Saint Croix, Cayuga, chasselas (a native Swiss variety), or a well-crafted Baco noir to a merlot (derived from the French *merle* meaning blackbird) or chardonnay (although there is a town of Chardonnay, the origin of the grape's name is surprisingly unclear as it may have originated in the town of Chablis!).

Flavor complexity can make a wine very interesting, and is a critically important factor in any fine, appropriately aged, well-crafted wine made from great grapes. Creating a fabulous wine that ages well to become complex, with interesting character on the palate and nose, is a dream of virtually every serious wine maker. Some grape types are better for this than others, and some of us prefer a variety of unique taste experiences to tradition flavors. Complexity and variety make wine interesting.

We were introduced to one perspective on wine varieties and flavor when we were invited to lunch at the home of an elderly couple. The very proper, eighty-six-year-old host had experienced great success as a New York City corporate attorney. He and his lovely wife lived very comfortably and could afford what they liked. They served two wines with an elegant luncheon, prepared by our hostess. I asked about the wines, and our host stated simply, "We serve only Bordeaux in this house."

Interesting, I thought. They were wonderful wines. But then it occurred to me that my hosts were missing out on so many other interesting wines from different places and of unique grape types. They simply loved Bordeaux wine, which is easy to understand. I do too, but have fun experiencing many different wines, prepared with unique techniques, from all kinds of grapes grown in their special, unique environments, properly balanced and well-made. French-American hybrids can yield interesting, delightful wines when grown and vinified well. Life is short, and the diversity of well made, interesting wines from a variety of grape types is exciting.

2004

Spring brought early warmth and pleasing dry weather. At the March Connecticut Vineyard and Winery Association meeting, some were concerned about trunk damage from the recent harsh winter and feared that some vines might not bear fruit.

I looked at our vines frequently as the days became longer and the sun warmer. Foch was first to return, with leaf buds abundant on all plants, but our cherished riesling lagged behind. Aside from a few shoots from the graft sites (which I had protected with soil cover the previous fall), the consecutive frigid winters had seriously impaired the riesling. By late June, I was cutting back vines that had matured over five years. All that was left was a series of small shoots from the base, which I nursed along. Fortunately, though, I had ordered some new riesling the previous fall, and we planted those vines the second week of May, in deep holes with a boost of manure, compost, and lots of water for each vine.

Foch was growing as if nothing had happened, and both the Cayuga and the Vidal blanc from 2003 were flourishing. They had weathered the brutal cold formidably. I mixed early sprays with a pungent fermented-salmon solution that had proven effective for keeping deer (and everyone else!) away the previous year. By mid-July, despite the sprays, powdery mildew was finding havens of shade and dampness in the vineyard. The canopy of leaves was thick from the past fall's fertilizer application, and this full foliage diminished air circulation, thus increasing dampness. To combat this, I sprayed some sulfur and removed many leaves as well as afflicted clusters of grapes to increase airflow around the vines. I subdued the powdery mildew after a battle.

The vineyard was, and is, my beautiful and seductive mistress. I was beginning to realize the commitment, and I loved it. I found time to work in the vineyard for thirty to forty minutes or so most days after work. This was enough to stay in touch with the vineyard's life.

I brought a bottle of our riesling to a summer barbecue hosted by friends, chilled it upon arriving at their home, and then, later, uncorked and shared it, along with some details about the process of raising grapes and making wine. They liked it—and that was all that mattered.

I noted little warty structures on the underside of Cayuga leaves and contacted a grape-growing friend, who made the diagnosis. The new culprit this season was grape-leaf phylloxera. Sprays for this troublesome little fly were said to be very toxic, so I removed as much of the smitten foliage as I could, hoping that interrupting their life cycle would be enough. Phylloxera is a worrisome infestation because it had destroyed European *vinifera* years earlier, but, as I learned from my reading online, the grape-leaf phylloxera we were seeing is different and is not likely to destroy vines as did the earlier, root-killing European variety. Later that fall, I spoke with a gentleman at the Connecticut Vineyard and Winery Association who suggested that a nontoxic oil spray the following year might prevent phylloxera infestation. I never implemented this and just kept pulling off the warty leaves, sending them away with our trash each week. I never used a toxic spray and at last check in 2016, the vines were fine.

The late season was much brighter in 2004—with better weather, more sun, and some warm days without humidity. The grapes did well—Foch, Cayuga, and some first-year Vidal blanc. The clusters continued to plump up, with colors that became steadily richer and deeper. The mildew and black rot were gone, and the days were cooler, limiting the possibility of another mildew invasion.

We harvested in the third week of September, on a balmy day. My friend Eric drove up from New Jersey; my neighbors Barbara and Dan helped; and Jerry, my retired-English-teacher friend, joined our picking crew. We picked all the Foch, washed and crushed it, and then covered the juice for chilling outside before we sat together for one of Lynn's beautiful dinners. I had bought some local seyval blanc wine, but the highlights were Lynn's cuisine and Eric's handcrafted wine—a rich, full-bodied, and complex cabernet blend of mature, imported California grapes that Eric had produced.

A week later, Lynn and I picked the small crop of Cayuga and Vidal blanc, crushed the grapes, chilled the must overnight, and then fermented it to a crisp and tasty endpoint. This was a twelve-gallon year.

Craig, a young orthopedic surgeon; and his wife, Shannon, stopped by for a taste of the 2003 Foch one colorful fall afternoon when the foliage was near its peak, ablaze with crimson and lemon-yellow leaves, in the hills around our home. A year in the bottle had helped the Foch a lot; the tannins were down a little, and so the Foch was slightly softer and more flavorful than it had been. Craig is one of the more enthusiastic, genuinely pleasant people I have ever known, which is indeed a blessing when serving full bodied Foch wine. Unlike my mother-in-law, who looked somewhat horrified upon tasting the full-bodied Foch, Craig and Shannon said they found the wine, after my full disclosure of its "unique, acquired taste" character, "interesting and enjoyable." We reveled in the New England fall day and the wine. The alcohol always helps!

In 2004, we put our Foch wine in a small American oak barrel that I had acquired through a group purchase by the Connecticut Vineyard and Winery Association. Everyone admonished, "Don't over oak," so I kept checking the taste of this batch of Foch after the first couple of months, "topping off" the wine (the barrel absorbs some water, and some wine evaporates) with small amounts of the previous season's wine. By about three months later, a faint "hint of oak" was notable, so I bottled the whole lot as well as a few bottles of the Cayuga and Vidal blanc—our first crops of these latter two grapes. It was very exciting to have our own white wine again, as the entire small batch of original riesling wine had been quickly consumed.

Late in the fall of 2004, we received a large complimentary delivery of aged horse manure from one of the operating-room aides, Rob, in exchange for letting him hunt deer on our property. I spread this rich, natural fertilizer generously around the vineyard to give the forthcoming 2005 season a boost.

2005

The winter of 2005 was tame. Spring came early, and I aggressively pruned all the vines in hopes of a limited crop and better overall quality. I had ordered twenty-five vines each of Cayuga and Saint Croix, so we dug fifty holes, replacing the nonproductive *vinifera* vines and blackberries that had proliferated in the middle of the vineyard. Two orthopedic salesmen, Ray and Brendan, visited one sunny spring morning on their motorcycles to help with the planting. After the planting, we all tasted some of the previous season's wine.

Warm weather brought premature buds and leaves that unfurled by mid-May on the heartier varieties (Cayuga and Foch). A rogue frost in late May decimated the tender young-vine growth, but warm weather persisted. The 2005 growth exploded nonetheless, with no evidence of the pesky grape-cane girdler that had damaged new growth the previous season. We had controlled this insect infestation by simply interrupting its life cycle, without chemicals. Even the Japanese beetles were light in 2005, and no deer damage occurred thanks to my coating the young vines early with fermented-salmon spray.

A woman of about fifty with Parkinson's disease came to my office because of shoulder problems and told me her Parkinson's had been caused by pesticides that were sprayed abundantly around the farm in South America where she had spent her childhood. She was sure of this and medical literature had shown that Parkinsonism is associated with pesticides(8). I had discovered that I could control insect problems by reading about them and then interrupting their life cycles or by simply removing them one at a time. Clipping off some leaves and new-growth tips here and there seemed like a great alternative, one that was practical in a small vineyard. We were happily using sustainable agriculture methods- interrupt the harmful insect's life cycle by understanding it instead of using toxic substances.

While walking through the vineyard one day, I spotted commotion at the adjacent blueberry patch. A moderately large bird, bigger than a crow, had caught its leg in the protective netting over our blueberries. Approaching the distressed bird, I could see that it was a falcon, with its beak wide open, ready to attack. Such birds of prey can snap the necks of small animals with their powerful beaks. I studied the bird's markings and then went into the house to find Lynn, a bird book, and a pair of scissors in order to cut the netting around its badly entangled leg. I would perform this rescue operation from the other side of the blueberry netting, hopefully a safe barrier against the somewhat large, threatening beak! The experience that followed was extraordinary.

As Lynn watched and studied the bird, determining that it was a merlin falcon, I slowly, carefully cut strands of blueberry netting around the bird's strangulated talon. The bird stood poised, beak open wide, watching the scissors, and my fingers. With each clip of the scissors, as the leg slowly became less encumbered, the falcon's beak relaxed; until its beak was completely closed when the leg finally fell free of the netting. At this point, the falcon sat there, motionless, looking at me and leading me to believe that it was too far gone to fly, probably, I thought, due to dehydration. It just sat there looking at me, and I at him (or her). As I turned slowly to walk away, the bird shot into the sky and sailed easily off across the road, then back over our heads; next, the bird swung wide and landed in a nearby tree on the one good leg.

After hearing the bird's cry and remembering that we had seen falcons chasing smaller birds around the fields (and away from our grapes) adjacent to the vineyard, Lynn and I studied the book together and again confirmed that the falcon was indeed a merlin.

Merlin falcons are known for their speed and hunting finesse; they are swifter than other birds on which they are known to prey. Sightings of merlins in our area were uncommon, but we established that merlins were known to be in the area from time to time. We hypothesized that this beautiful bird had swooped down on a small creature, maybe a bird or mouse, looking for sustenance that day, only to become entangled by our almost-invisible blueberry netting.

The next day, Lynn took her mother to the Beardsley Park Zoo in Bridgeport for an outing and spoke with the aviary keeper there about our merlin experience. The bird expert thought that, in spite of the severe leg damage, the bird would likely survive.

The following year, 2006, we realized that merlins had returned to our vineyard and were chasing smaller birds around the fields behind our house. By this time, we could recognize their shrill cry. The 2006 season also brought new falcon life to the vineyard, as our pair of merlins gave birth to their young in a nearby tree, fledging these fluffy, young, screeching birds on the trellising wires of our vineyard! These young merlins would dance around also on the posts of the vineyard, seeming to call for their mother as they stumbled in search of food. The swift ability of the parent falcons to grasp small birds in flight contrasted dramatically with the movements of these awkward young birds of prey. At one point, one of the merlins attacked a full-grown turkey behind our house—feathers flying everywhere, but no clear sign of victory, just testimony to the bold determination of the adult merlin falcon—maybe a one-legged merlin! In 2006, after hearing the merlin's piercing cries over our vineyard a few times, we named our vineyard "Merlin Meadows."

Lynn was inspired by this experience and worked steadily on a merlin wine-bottle label, applying her trained watercolor-painting hand to create a special design. With the help of a graphic-artist friend, a beautiful label for our wine was born, depicting a lone merlin flying gracefully and protectively over a ying-yang configuration of our balanced grape vines.

The remaining 2005 summer brought very little rain and generally warm temperatures. The harvest was abundant, with both Phoebe and Brad home joining my sommelier friend, Eric, and his wife, Candace, for the harvest. Friends stopped by to observe, drink wine, pick grapes, or all three.

Eric and Patrick, a couple of young guys who aspired to opening a brewery someday, had planted cascade hops in a section of our vineyard earlier in the season. We nursed their baby hops and enjoyed watching them grow. In just a couple of months, these vigorous hops plants established feet in our soil and were growing rapidly. The following year we had a nice little harvest of cascade hops that Eric and Patrick brewed into a unique fresh-hop beer. A few years later, Patrick went to school in Germany and became a *braumeister* (brewmaster), following in the footsteps of his maternal grandfather. He and Eric then went on to open a popular brewery in Richmond, Virginia, which they named Hardywood.

We foot-crushed our Foch grapes that year, washing our feet adjacent to the crushing tub so that we could step directly into the bin of grapes. Stomping on grape skins in a large plastic tub turned out to be challenging, as grape skins are as slippery as fresh oysters! Fortunately, no one fell into (or out of) the crushing vat, but some of the upper-body contortions necessary to stay upright were good entertainment that day along with banjo and mandolin music provided by friends Mike and Al.

The 2005 harvest yielded twenty-seven gallons of juice—mostly Cayuga. We used large jugs of ice to cold stabilize all the juice overnight (to prevent any bacterial or unwanted yeast activity) and started all fermentations the following morning. Many wine makers consider a brix of 18 to be ideal for Foch wine, and that was right where our brix was. Cayuga wine also tastes better if picked at a brix of 18, and that too was where the Cayuga grapes were.

We discovered a new, and better, way to make Foch wine—no skins and stems, just ferment the juice. This produced a rich blush wine that reminded us of Beaujolais, so we called it "Foch Beaujolais," and this wine, with its faint background flavor of cotton candy, was then confirmed to be our preferred style of wine for Foch grapes.

By late 2005, we had racked the Cayuga a couple of times and bottled some of it. The flavor of our pure Cayuga wine was similar to sauvignon blanc, we thought, with overtones of citrus and a pleasant, slightly metallic character, but still with a little more acid than ideal. I shared tastes with my assistant, Donna, and with one of the orthopedic-surgery residents who brought in a bottle of his homemade amarone wine, rich with a character of raisins and dark chocolate. The contrast of citrusy white wine with dense, chocolaty red wine was intriguing, not to mention a great way to end a day in the office. One of the special pleasures of growing grapes and making wine is sharing it.

The year 2005 had been a very good one, and I hoped for a resurgence of riesling in 2006, particularly as I had originally thought that riesling would be our premier grape. Cayuga, however, was the undisputed winner, at that time, for our climate and soil. It was the right fit for our terroir. Riesling never flourished in our cool New England climate. Meanwhile, the new Saint Croix plantings offered hope of a first-rate, cold-hardy red grape. Our recently discovered "Foch Beaujolais" technique was an encouraging prelude to the anticipated abundant 2006 Foch harvest.

The winter was mild compared to other years, with very little snow. It was so warm in January that we worried about premature sprouting of new-grape-vine growth, but this did not occur even by April 1, when the weather improved dramatically. The temperatures kept moving upward, and daffodils bloomed well before any buds swelled on our vines. By that time, though, when the nights were cold and the days were warm, sap was running out the cut ends of the carefully pruned vines, just as sap was rising in maple trees and maple sugaring was at its best. The natural world was coming back to life as spring arrived in early April 2006.

CONNECTION

Never did sun more beautifully steep
In his first splendor, valley, rock, or hill;
Ne'er saw I, never felt, a calm so deep!

Wrote William Wordsworth in "Composed upon Westminster Bridge" (1802). As he considered the "beauty of the morning," Wordsworth's words sang of the harmony found upon viewing the "fields and sky all bright and glittering in the smokeless air."

What is this allure, this mystery and beauty, we feel in nature? Could it be that we are "hardwired" to connect with the natural world? To survive, our predecessors felt they had to subdue the world in which they lived. Today, this has changed for those of us who find a strong aesthetic sense of meaning upon viewing and appreciating the beauty, balance, and wonders of our natural world while trying to understand the vagaries of humanity in order to survive. Today, fields, streams, gardens, oceans, mountains, and landscapes provide refuge from human struggles in an increasingly technological world. We need the land and it's balance, and must connect with it, and care for it.

In fact, as Aldo Leopold said: "it is inconceivable to me that an ethical relation to the land can exist without love, respect and admiration for land, and a high regard for its value." (9)

John Pryor Fulkerson

William Wordsworth grew up in an affluent family in rural Cumberland County, England, along the beautiful Derwent River and spent many childhood hours exploring the depths and beauty of it and the surrounding English countryside. He loved walking and, when he was eighteen years old, spent an entire summer hiking around his beloved Cumberland landscape. Later, he trekked through mainland Europe. His gift was writing poetry, and his legacy is, in large part, an indelible verbal expression of this wondrous natural world in which he grew up. These lines from William Wordsworth's "Tintern Abbey" are rife with immersion in and understanding of Nature's intrigue wherein we find:

> ...that blessed mood,
> In which the burthen of the mystery,
> In which the heavy and the weary weight
> Of all this unintelligible world,
> Is lightened:—that serene and blessed mood,
> In which the affections gently lead us on,—
> Until, the breath of this corporeal frame
> And even the motion of our human blood
> Almost suspended, we are laid asleep
> In body, and become a living soul:
> While with an eye made quiet by the power
> Of harmony, and the deep power of joy,
> We see into the life of things.

We may be fortunate to find this connection, so aptly expressed by William Wordsworth, in garden and vineyard. Perhaps it is the completeness of the vineyard experience. Vines, stark and bare in the early spring, soon flourish with new growth, which quickly take in sunlight through beckoning leaves to photosynthesize (turning sunlight into sugar); climb eagerly; and later produce taut, full clusters of grapes for the harvest. The amazing internal machinery of each vine processes sunlight and water with nutrients from the soil to produce sweet fruit. Our best contributions are to help sunlight get to the leaves by keeping down excessive foliage, assuring that nutrients are available in sufficient but not-too-abundant quantities, keeping the canopy open to air circulation (pruning and stripping leaves as needed), warding off invaders, and staying out of the way while the vines do their magnificent work:

> With an eye made quiet by the power
> of harmony, and the deep power of joy,
> we see into the life of things. (Wordsworth)

In sustainable agriculture, natural processes work to our benefit if we understand the behaviors of unwanted intruders and how to interrupt their patterns and plans, by identifying invasive bugs and growths, devising ways of defeating them—understanding how they live and then figuring out how to disrupt their cycles of life in the vineyard. Birds and "good" insects are natural predators that will eliminate many destructive pests, so we foster their well being by avoiding chemicals that can harm them. At times, we may step in and alter the life cycle of some destructive insects such that they vanish completely without using any chemical. As mentioned earlier in this story, it is possible to eliminate grape-cane girdlers (which clip off new growth of grape vines) by simply removing the damaged growth where they are known to leave their eggs. One can live with a few Japanese beetles by limiting the population manually and may even discover that a controlled number of Japanese beetles helps a vineyard by thinning the foliage a little, opening up the canopy to allow more air and sunlight to wash over grapes. Removing warty, infested grape leaves and disposing of them in trash that goes off the property controls potential multiple generations of grape leaf phylloxera that can quickly evolve in one's vineyard. Thus, "sustainable" grape growing requires maintenance of a healthy self-regulating environment, without using insecticide.

Sustainability is inherent in a balanced natural world. The harmony of which William Wordsworth speaks resonates with balance, and this becomes possible upon overcoming its obstacles. Grapevines are good at overcoming adversity. They can tolerate drought better than many other fruits and vegetables as their roots extend deep into the earth seeking nutrients and water. Grapevines incorporate and reveal the resounding harmony, generosity, and abundance that is present around us.

Speaking of harmony, Mike, Jerry, and I gathered with our stringed instruments over Lynn's chili and corn bread. We had all played in small folk groups at one time or another. Jerry and I could sing and play guitars. Jerry could harmonize and we knew many of the same tunes—some Kingston Trio, Woody Guthrie, Appalachian folk songs, and assorted other such music of that genre that was popular in the 1960s. Harmony is what connected us— harmony of purpose, in our friendships and in the music itself. More recently, I was talking with my friend Ted, a former college classmate who happened to be studying music theory at the time. We talked about sound and resonance, rhythm and harmony—about how these affect mood and spirit. Ted (who plays the drums) pointed out that the beat in a lot of music is similar to a heartbeat, and how this powers the music. Music may draw one to touch what is divine at times, where the vague line between heaven and earth becomes less distinct. Peace and wonder dwell in this place. Like music, the lush beauty of a well-tended vineyard and its wine may evoke a similar sense of connection and wonder in which the power of harmony and the bounty of nature merge.

2006

The balance of vineyard life was healthy in 2006, with a diversity of hungry birds flying through the vineyard, patrolling for insects but unable to reach our grapes through abundant netting, as the grapes matured.

But as we celebrated our progress and the health of our vineyard, the rainy deluge of 2006 began, seriously disrupting the spontaneity and harmonious progress of our vineyard with black rot and mildew. As I used sulfur sprays at two-week intervals, everything seemed secure except our Foch, which a sulfur-resistant type of mildew had again afflicted. Black rot was also attacking the vineyard again. Weed and vine growth exploded, reducing airflow enough that dampness got trapped around our grapes, providing a comfortable home for dreaded mildew and black rot. I had fallen behind so easily, perhaps seduced by the early signs of success in our vineyard.

I knew that I was facing a war, and so I spent hours feverishly evaluating each vine and then, again, removing all the infected foliage, sick clusters, weeds, and excessive vine growth—spraying more thoroughly than ever, using sprays appropriate for black rot and mildew, in a struggle to salvage the remaining grapes. I called a professor of viticulture whom I had met at a vineyard association meeting and he stopped by for a visit and also to taste our previous year's vintage. His response was clear and unrelenting; he gave me the insight and encouragement that I desperately needed. "Cut!" he said.

John Pryor Fulkerson

One look around after his visit, and I realized how relaxed I had been, letting vines touch the ground while I enjoyed sunny days off, assuming that our healthy vineyard would thrive in this long growing season! I had to catch up.

My professor friend taught me a hard lesson that day as he went out of his way to visit on a precious Sunday afternoon, not to taste 1989 Bordeaux, but to sample and take home some of our 2005 Merlin Meadows Cayuga with my thanks for his generous expertise!

Right after his visit, I dressed for hard work and entered the vineyard for hours of cutting and hauling. Finally, I looked at the vineyard and saw sunlight passing through and under the vines. No vines drooped near the ground and now I could see many remaining clusters that had previously been engulfed in excessive growth, noting a gentle breeze passing through the vineyard as I walked along the rows.

A small crop survived the rains of July and August, and leaf phylloxera was less abundant, thankfully, than in 2005. Our daughter Phoebe traveled from Colorado for the harvest and spent some time at the end of one day painting landscapes near our vineyard. Grandma was home for the harvest also, happy to sit in the vineyard sorting out immature grape clusters as the rest of us picked grapes to "It's Amore" wafting from the nearby CD player one beautiful, sunny New England autumn afternoon. As we picked, the brimming buckets went into the back of our well-worn 1973 Jeep CJ5. Next they were transported to the rear of the house, and thence crushed and pressed so that their juices could be transported to the wine room and chilled. We combined the Cayuga and Vidal blanc since the harvest was small, and I pressed the Foch grapes immediately, in an attempt to reproduce the nice blush wine of the previous year by fermenting Foch juice without stems and skins. After chilling the juice overnight (cold stabilization) and adjusting both acid and sugar, I added yeast and the fermentations started promptly—creating eleven gallons this year. It seemed such a small production from so many vines, but for this home vintner, the first taste of the new wine made it all worthwhile.

2007

Blooming heathers appeared in January, as spring seemed to be arriving in the heart of winter. Ladybugs gathered on windowpanes and darted across our living room in the passive solar heat of this south-facing room. Then, in February, the temperatures plummeted to negative twenty, with no snow on the ground, before normal winter weather returned. The overall winter precipitation (snow) was well below normal, so the vine trunks and remaining grafts were vulnerable to the arctic onslaught of winter 2007. I knew I would be cutting back our vines rigorously once again anyway, as they had already suffered damage from 2006 black rot and mildew, and I feared another harsh blow—further damage to our bare vines from frigid temperatures.

In March, the wines of 2006 were ready to test and bottle. The Cayuga was crisp and flavorful. The Saturday of Easter weekend, we were invited to a friend's home for dinner, and we presented our 2004 Foch red wine, aged in oak, and a bottle of the flavorful 2006 Merlin Meadows Vidal-Cayuga white. Our little group of friends gravitated repeatedly to the Vidal-Cayuga—it didn't matter that the Foch, while palatable, was slow to disappear. This was no surprise. They liked the Cayuga!

The 2007 growing season started quietly as temperatures rose steadily after May 1. Just about the right amount of rain fell, and deer seemed to be scarce, so the tender new vines grew safely and steadily. The only mishap occurred when Lynn opened the barn door and felt something "like a thick piece of rope or a garage-door spring" fall onto her head, then to her shoulder, and finally onto the ground. When she looked down, it was a large snake! The snake wiggled away quickly. About a week later, as I opened the door, that same snake (I assume) fell down again. I almost jumped out of my pants. We must have scared the snake, because we never saw him again after that. Maybe he saw me reaching for a large shovel as he shot away into the bushes!

Because of the previous season's mildew debacle, I sprayed regularly and followed the professor's advice, cutting out all the "bull canes" (nonproductive, large, long, shadowing vines). This kept the understory (beneath the lowest wire) open to air flow. Cultivating the soil under our vines kept down weeds and grass so that air streamed freely under and through the vines. Hence mildew and black rot were scarce—another small victory and lesson learned.

Other than some turkeys fluffing around in the newly tilled earth, presumably looking for bugs and stealing a few green berries, wildlife was not a problem, and the grapevines grew steadily and abundantly. My worthy opponents—deer, turkeys, birds of all sorts (particularly starlings and brown thrashers), grape-leaf phylloxera, grape-cane girdler beetles, flea beetles, mildew, black rot, ants, yellow jackets, drought, hail, excessive rain, and so on—were not done with us yet! I had never used an insecticide and didn't want to.

Eight years from its inception, our vineyard was healthy. Seeing bees, both bumble and honey, buzzing through the vineyard reminded me again of the harmony there. Grapes are self-pollinating, so they don't need bees. Bees were all around, nonetheless, seeming to enjoy the healthy vineyard environment and its adjacent flower beds (including roses at the end of each row of the vineyard), daylilies, sunflowers and clover. Birds would swoop through the vineyard regularly and presumably found what they sought—little bugs—from time to time. We had nesting boxes in several locations and found bluebirds, in particular, flying into two of them. Swallows and purple martins would sail around the fields and through the vineyard. Life was balanced and abundant. The soil was rich with earthworms and thousands of microbial organisms doing their work. Occasionally we would spot a fox or coyote hunting in the fields, and birds of prey, particularly red-tailed hawks, watched the fields and vineyard from above.

But some leaves indicated a return of grape-leaf phylloxera and removal of infected leaves, particularly on the Cayuga, reduced productivity. In addition, tiny ants were battling at the tips of some new growth. I removed these areas and discarded them with our trash. Yellow jackets were abundant, landing on single grapes to drill a hole and drink the sweet juice of our grapes. A few yellow-jacket traps, filled with sugary apple juice, kept them under control.

Meanwhile, it was time to free up the last five-gallon carboy and get ready for what looked like a very promising harvest. I had bottled the previous season's Foch Beaujolais, our best yet, so all the carboys were ready for new wine!

Anticipating a larger-than-usual harvest, I purchased a fifty-liter, stainless steel fermentation container to supplement the remodeled beer keg contributed by my beer-making friends, Patrick and Eric.

This season had yielded an abundance of tasty wild blackberries, raspberries, and blueberries on our property. Many of these went promptly into the freezer to brighten our breakfast cereal with their antioxidant powers the following winter, but we also carried large numbers of them from vine to breakfast table within minutes of harvest. Lynn also transformed berries into hearty jams; compotes; and sweet, mouth-watering sauces for ice cream and other selected delicacies.

In August 2007, Lynn's vegetable garden was bursting with plump, well-rounded eggplants; long, crisp green beans to nibble right at the time of picking; deep, blood-red beets and their "ready to sauté" beet greens; a variety of wavy, flavorful lettuces; sweet and firey hot peppers; bold, long zucchini squashes; full-flavored, plump, juicy tomatoes to be eaten, from time to time, in the garden with a bit of salt or later cooked down into hearty sauce for the future; shiny, green basil; wispy cilantro; and wonderfully flavorful new potatoes.

Our grapes began to plump up and look increasingly healthy. I dispatched the minimal mildew with sulfur, and the race to harvest was on. So the netting went up, and we watched as the grapes became plumper and plumper, richer and richer; the days, shorter; and the evenings, cooler.

After netting the vines, we sat back a little. During this time, our daughter won an art competition and was pronounced the festival artist for the Steamboat Springs International Wine Festival, so off we went to share this joyous occasion with her! In addition to seeing her and her artwork honored, we tasted many wines at the event; took a couple of short wine-appreciation courses; and savored the Rocky Mountains under vibrant, clear blue skies with our daughter. We named our 2006 Cayuga Merlin Meadows Steamboat Picker's Reserve in her honor, as she had helped pick the grapes also. Another bottle, which we donated to the event's silent auction, sold for fifty dollars!

Brad rallied his best friends to pick grapes. Additionally, our neighbor Mike and his friends from Vermont wanted to pick grapes, as did a few of my friends. Our happy pickers, ages thirty to seventy-five, were eager to join the traditional picking, eating, and wine-drinking event.

Lynn and I had started the picking early because of an impending frost, and we had collected enough to start a batch of Saint Croix wine fermenting before the main harvest weekend in late September 2007. The frost never came, and all the remaining grapes stayed intact. I set up a new, efficient harvest plan for the remaining grapes because of an anticipated plentiful 2007 yield. We would pick and pick and pick until our collecting bins were full in the back of the jeep, and then we would drive all the grapes to an open area behind the house for washing, sorting, crushing, and pressing in one continuous process before going out for further harvest. We did this over and over until the last grapes had been crushed, pressed, and carried into the wine room.

On Saturday morning at about eleven o'clock, Lynn brought out some of the previous year's vintage and a tray of glasses! "Wine at eleven a.m.?" I asked. Yet this was Lynn's stroke of genius. Our picker friends and family loved it as the wine flowed steadily on that day of picking, laughter, and wine making. This seemed a little bacchanalian!

The joyful time we spent together was made more meaningful by the abundant harvest. This time would be relived, as its wine would be available on our wine racks for years to come, a reminder of the friendship, family, and joy of those precious moments working together to make wine, cradled in the abundance of nature. New life on the vine yields not only a product for consumption, but also a lasting reminder of unifying time with others and the uniqueness of that year's struggles and victories in the vineyard, without which there would be no harvest.

John Pryor Fulkerson

The Possibility of Completion

Some interactions touch the possibility of completion
in the turns of daily life—
wind and sail,
paint and canvas,
pen and paper,
match and kindling.

With the battery connected at both poles,
the engine starts,
as moving waters merge at the sea.

To the tune of fiddle, guitar, and mandolin, we pressed out over seventy gallons of grape juice in 2007. The wine was prepared without oak, and some of the Foch grape juice was again fermented in the style of white wine—no skins, while the remaining Foch was fermented on its skins in the typical red wine tradition. With the long, warm growing season, the grapes had reached greater maturity and higher sugar content than in the past, so I added less sugar to the must (grape juice). Richer, more full-bodied grape juice with just the right amount of acid was ready for fermentation.

In late December, I racked this wine a second time and took a few bottles of the newly clarified wine to share with my surgical team. They brought in cheeses, breads, and sausages for the event. As the first major snowstorm of the year fell that afternoon, we were "snowed in"—with wine and food! The spirit of this event took on a special quality in the storm as everyone spent plenty of time tasting and talking—until snow had been cleared from the roads and a fresh pot of coffee provided support for the drive home.

The very abundant 2007 harvest produced much wine. Lynn's Merlin Meadows label was not quite ready, so we designed and ordered some pro forma labels online, put some of these on bottles of wine, and started giving the previous year's wine to friends in view of the pending large volume of wine on our shelves. The abundance of wine made our decisions about gifts easy, and we were also given an opportunity to serve our wine at a fundraising event in May 2008. One event attendee asked if she could buy it. I loved this but responded that we couldn't sell it because of federal regulations. She gave me her phone number anyway!

The wine was very good in 2007, so we consumed it and gave it away. Fast forward to 2017, I found a lonely bottle of our 2007 Marechal Foch in a dusty corner of the wine room. Early in its life, I had set the bottle aside, or forgotten about it, apparently. We opened it with little expectation of anything great. I sniffed the cork to be sure it hadn't gone bad over the years. Then we poured a small amount to test, and to our delight, the wine had a beautiful bouquet.

Lynn and I were very surprised by how good this wine was. The tannins had softened; the wine had developed a lush character, quite different from what we remembered of the young Foch; and we savored its richness and round smoothness. If only I had kept ten bottles of this wine on the shelf. I understood again that making and appreciating wine requires patience, time, and much experience.

2008

We bottled our 2007 wine in the late spring of 2008 using buckets, pitchers, and a funnel. The corker got gummed up, so I took it apart, and after tinkering with it for an hour or so, it was working smoothly again.

We planted ten Baco noir vines to further supplement our red-wine production, and then turned our attention to tiling the wine room floor, over the stark, gray cement that had been stained with blotches of spilled wine. It was tempting to leave these stains as memories of the early years, but we decided to proceed with tiles, which greatly improved the ambiance of our winemaking environment.

In late September 2008, Brad and his friends arrived for the harvest. We removed all the bird netting the third weekend of September, and fourteen of us picked, washed, crushed, and pressed grapes for two days. Lynn kept the food and wine flowing. The sun had a soft, autumn warmth and sparkle that glistened from the newly harvested grape clusters overflowing large bins in the back of our old, pea-green jeep. Some of the more energetic pickers took breaks to run, bike, or swim in the pond.

Conversation in the vineyard tends to be easy—ideas and stories flowing naturally through the vines. New friendships form quickly, and old friendships become stronger around grape leaves and fragrant full grape clusters. At a bonfire by the pond that evening, we continued conversations while toasting marshmallows; playing guitar; and singing under a clear, starry sky. We had shared the joy of working together, and now the newly prepared grape juice was chilling in our wine room, awaiting fermentation.

By the end of the weekend, fifty-five gallons of new wine were fermenting. This was particularly exciting in 2008, as we had found special GRE and D254 yeasts for the Foch and Saint Croix, respectively. After adding a malo-lactic treatment to some of the fermentations, the early Foch tasted pretty good with less acidity and a particularly nice flavor, likely a result of the Foch-specific GRE yeast. This year's vintage promised to be the best yet.

I pulled out a few of the less productive vines to make room for thirty-six new ones (Cayuga, traminette, and Saint Croix), which I would order for 2009.

After we had transferred all the fermenting wine to glass carboys with air locks, Lynn and I traveled to South Africa, where we were introduced to lions, cheetahs, leopards, rhinoceroses, hippopotamuses, water buffalo, baboons, violet-crested rollers, bee eaters, hyenas, and jackals (to name a few) at Mashatu Game Preserve (in Botswana) and Sabi Sands (Londolozi Game Preserve). Then we went on to visit Stellenbosch, a prime grape growing and wine-producing region in South Africa. Their white wines, particularly sauvignon blanc, were widely available and inexpensive. Most exciting, though, was the native South African pinotage wine, its grape having originated in Stellenbosch—a hybrid of pinot noir and hermitage grapes—thus the name pinotage. Abraham Izak Perold, the first professor of viticulture at Stellenbosch University, created pinotage in 1925. He planted his original hybrid seeds and then moved away before making wine from the grapes. Fortunately, others knew of the special hybrid plantings and cultivated them. The first production of wine from these plantings was some fifteen years later!

When we returned from our trip, several of the fermentations had stopped, and the yeast was settling. All fifty-five gallons were secure in glass carboys with air locks for a long winter rest. What could we do to make our wine even better? We were still learning...

2009

A dry, warm spring was just right for planting new grape vines. In early May, we planted twelve Cayuga, twelve traminette, and twelve Saint Croix vines. Around this time, I bottled the Saint Croix from 2008 (thirty-six bottles of this precious vintage) and received favorable reviews from friends and family. Maybe it was luck, the soil, the year, the D254 yeast, or bits of all of these. I had learned how to make good wine. We put the Saint Croix wine aside in our cool wine room to age and then experienced a very, very wet finish of the 2009 spring. We approached this challenging year prepared to prevent mildew and black rot by keeping the canopy wide open by pruning rigorously to allow ever more airflow and optimal access of sun to sweep away and evaporate dampness.

The rain was merciless. The grapes of one fellow vintner ten miles east of us were beaten by hail that punched holes in his new grape leaves. We never received this wrath of hail. The rain was almost constant through June and early July, so I kept up the sprays and made sure the canopy stayed open. The battle with weeds was constant. Bob, Marie, Brad, Mike, and I all put in many hours pulling weeds and tilling the soil. Turkeys came around in mid-July, peering at the new, green grape clusters, sometimes jumping up vertically to snatch a few. We just chased them away, except for two large males that stood their ground one evening. As I ran toward them, they turned and trod—slowly—away.

The Connecticut Vineyard and Winery Association met in Goshen, Connecticut in mid-July 2009. Bill Nail spoke about balancing vines to allow enough, but not too much, foliage to support the clusters of grapes on each vine—a challenging task, as it is foliage that absorbs sunlight to make sugar for the grapes through photosynthesis, yet too much foliage creates a damp, shady, unhealthy environment. Also, with too many clusters, the sugar levels might never become adequate to make good wine. "Dropping clusters" is hard to do (throwing away young fruit), but it is necessary in the grape-growing process so that available sugar will concentrate in the remaining grapes. Limiting the number of grape clusters per vine is essential in optimizing grape quality. This allows a concentration of the plant's energy, enhancing the sugar and flavor of the remaining grapes. Each vine can only support, optimally, a moderate number of grapes. Allowing too many grapes per vine is known as "overcropping."

I was fortunate to have lunch that day with a local commercial grape grower and his son. They spoke of balanced pruning of their seven thousand vines! My two hundred vines suddenly seemed more manageable. George and his son "make all the cuts." I understand this. Pruning is part of the art of viticulture—one that I did not fully appreciate in my earlier experience, but one that I came to value as an important part of my role in making our wine optimal. In general, when we look at great vineyards, we do not see too much foliage. Look at an uncontrolled vineyard, and the contrast is striking. Human hands must control the vigor of grape vines in order to produce the best harvest possible. In large vineyards, machines with huge, fanlike, vertical spinning cutters remove excessive foliage, but in most small vineyards, the vintner makes the cuts by hand.

Vines that drop down must be brought up, by hand, onto wires in the desired trellis pattern, or else they must be removed. With fewer clusters on the vine, the energy and nutrients will be channeled more effectively to remaining clusters. Each vine is treated specifically for its own needs, with balanced pruning always to optimize the grapes—fewer on each vine being better for quality and sugar content of the final product. This is why some small production vineyards can produce exceptional, unique wines.

John Pryor Fulkerson

In the summer of 2009, I submitted a bottle of our 2008 Saint Croix for an American Wine Society competition, not knowing that my Saint Croix, grown and made without oak in Connecticut, would be competing against wine made by Connecticut vintners using California cabernet sauvignon, then aged in oak barrels. California grapes get a lot more sun and have a much longer time on the vine because of the long growing seasons there, so their sugar levels typically run much higher, the acids lower. This produces a different character of wine, one that is rich with color and flavor. The bold richness of California cabernet has been rightfully extolled by Robert Parker, *Wine Spectator* columnists, and other authorities, because it *is* great, rich wine packed with flavor and aroma. Connecticut Saint Croix is different—dense and nutty but with a less abundant character compared to the dense fruit and richness of cabernets and merlots from warm climates; it is hard to compare such wines side by side. We didn't win any ribbon that day!

In 2009, we produced forty-seven gallons of wine. The early-summer rain had badly hurt the Saint Croix, and we ended up with one lonely five-gallon carboy of our beloved Saint Croix, which I blended with a small crop of Baco noir, since I didn't have enough Baco for a separate fermentation anyway. We also had our usual abundance of Foch and plenty of white wine (blended Cayuga and Vidal blanc), some of which I exchanged with a friend for apple butter and baked goods! Brad and friends arrived again for the harvest, largely the same group that harvested in 2008. After running and biking vigorously Saturday morning, they picked, crushed, pressed, drank, picked, drank, ate, picked, crushed, and drank until we had it all done in a matter of hours!

Lynn and I biked in Puglia, Italy, in the fall of 2009, after the fermentations were done and secured in the cool wine room. We experienced several different wines in Puglia, including negroamaro and malvasia, two of the grape types grown in southeastern Italy. We also tasted, for the first time, wine made from the fiano grape of southern Italy.

In Italy,
when the crowd turned,
we went to distant parts—
to the quiet of ancient-stone and stucco warmth,
espresso and Adriatic simplicity,
where Brunelleschi marble richness
filled an abundant afternoon.

I thought of Alice Feiring's book (5), realizing how much we enjoyed the Italian wines made from unusual grapes that reflected the character of soil, sun, and climate there. Could these wines win a competition against chardonnay from Burgundy? It just doesn't matter. What was, and is, most alluring about the Puglian wines was their uniqueness, reminding us of the light, fruitful chasselas white wine that we had loved in Switzerland on the shores of Lake Lausanne. It is simple, beautiful, and subtle, carrying with it, like the malvasia of Puglia, a really unique quality that I still seek (I have only found chasselas once, in New York City, since returning from our trip to Switzerland about a decade prior to this writing). Some wines are just unique, and as such, have special qualities that are intriguing and desirable.

Seltzer and lime? Can seltzer and lime be as great as rich sweetened lemonade? Or Coca-Cola? Many of us have tastes for each, at different times, and if there is going to be a competition, I would like to see colas against colas, seltzer and limes against seltzer and limes, and lemonade against lemonade! Better still, forget the competition and enjoy the diversity. The tall glass of lemonade, freshly made from ripe lemons, served on ice with just the right amount of sweetening on a hot summer day, is heavenly! And seltzer and lime before dinner with some appetizers may be just right for that time. Lemonade might not work as well, for many of us, with brie cheese, but some might love it! Some wines are luscious and unique, fermented with naturally occurring yeasts from their places of origin, reflecting the very nature of those terroirs. Many skilled vintners, on the other hand, emphasize using selected yeasts, careful barrel fermentation, special techniques, or whatever it takes to unveil some of the most wonderful, mysterious, and rich qualities of individual grape types. Perhaps some purists would say that a steak should be cooked without any alteration of the meat in order to get a full sense of that steak, prepared in its own juices, while another steak lover might advocate marinating and grilling over a mesquite-wood fire to maximize what the steak has to offer by conferring subtle qualities to the final product. Both are great!

It makes sense to get the best out of grapes. Isn't this analogous to what a great chef does? He or she gets the freshest and best ingredients and prepares a dish designed to bring out the best, whether it is fish, chicken, beef, vegetables, or something else. But then there is a place for an outstanding piece of fish, simply broiled with lemon and butter—yet even these are additives.

I like the idea of growing the best possible grapes in well prepared soil; adding nutrients to the soil *to optimize what the soil can do for the grapes*; using good wine-making techniques, including the best, most appropriate yeast (instead of casting the lot of a wine to the fate of an arbitrary wild yeast); adjusting the acid content up front as needed; and then letting the natural process take over to work its magic on the grape juice of a given terroir. This is the allure, beauty and intrigue of making wine.

John Pryor Fulkerson

Faint Vapor

At the first sense of stagnation,
I opened some windows.
The fresh breeze was light and warm,
so I sat with eyes closed
feeling the air,
then walked where integration led,
love's passion employed.
The crimson dawn resonated,
faint vapor
circling up from the sea,
combing slowly along the shore
and arousing curiosity
about each element of the new day.

Fortunately I met one
who would linger long afternoons
over Wordsworth and tea—
no chatter, no miscalculated idleness;
just broad paint strokes.

It appeared that we would see a lot of Foch red wine, from the most abundant of all grape types planted on our property, in subsequent years. Initially, I just adjusted the Foch juice brix to a suitable level, and let it ferment on its deep, dark, purple-red skins. I decided not to dilute the juice for fear of diminishing the Foch wine's flavor. And we did get flavor—lots of it! This was a dense, dark purple-red wine with high alcohol, and…high acid, as well as the true flavor of full-bodied, foxy Foch! Our friends and family were gracious and tried hard to be complimentary. Friends are great that way, and I soaked up every favorable word, until I accepted the truth: this wine wasn't very good.

I eventually learned that one should only bring one's very best wine to the taste of a friend. I made mistakes repeatedly in this area—hastily pulling a random bottle off the rack when a friend stopped by, only to find some bits of tarnished grape skin floating in the glass poured, or a bitter taste. *As far as the other person is concerned, every bit of your wine is as good as what you just served.* Now we only serve the very best available. Our very best wine is the "reserve" ---and we always have some reserved for friends.

We shared a bottle of our Saint Croix with friends on their fortieth anniversary, having put together a little dinner party for this special occasion. We placed high hopes on this bottle, particularly since it was a very new (four months from harvest) red and was from our second crop of Saint Croix. Because it was a special occasion, we tasted the wine formally, and the result was uniform. The Saint Croix passed muster and started off a relaxed and lighthearted evening. Unlike the first bottles of Foch we served, this wine had been prepared after years of experience, carefully selected yeast, precise adjustment of acid and sugar, and a desire to serve our friends the best we could produce. We were proud of our wine that evening.

I looked for opportunities to exchange wine. One of the nurses at our surgery center wanted some white wine (her husband makes red wine). I saw her almost every morning I was there, and was happy to bring her a bottle of Vidal-Cayuga and grateful to subsequently receive a bottle of her husband's red wine, made from imported California grapes, which we enjoyed with an Italian dinner at home one evening.

In the course of conversations, other interesting wine barter occurred. One of my friends, a surgical technician in eastern Connecticut, raises mules and offered to deliver a truckload of manure. Not wanting to accept payment, I offered the alternative of an exchange for wine. Later she produced some dandelion wine, so we exchanged again. Next, I found a neighbor who offered washed, label-free wine bottles in exchange for wine. We continued to find interesting and enjoyable ways to manage our abundance. A load of manure arrived from another friend Tom, and he went home with a much lighter case of Merlin Meadows wine. Some friends who work with me at our surgical center traveled to New York State and spotted Fulkerson wine (from the Fulkerson vineyard on Lake Seneca), so they gave me a couple of bottles, and I, in turn, gave them each a bottle of our latest Cayuga.

Fortunately for those of us who tend vineyards with care, the return is often plentiful. Like people, vineyards manifest all sorts of imperfections and idiosyncrasies, yet we still love them. No vineyard is without blemishes and quirks—soil depletion, inadequate air flow, pests, intruders, mildew, too dry, too much shade, too wet, and so on. In tending a vineyard, the grower must spend time and effort becoming aware of the tarnishes of the beloved vineyard, and then care for them, in spite of the flaws and challenges. The results then, year after year, are satisfying—not perfect by any means, but satisfying. When the care fails, the defective vine is pulled and a new one planted. Not all vines will survive.

Blemishes and Quirks

I love the fresh-baked-cookie-scented days of childhood,
clean salt air wafting by,
worldly cares pausing
where intellect and dreams run hand in hand
far from crowded, intoxicating corners
packed with urchins of self-deprecation.

Once love's fine crystal
rolled off its table and struck the floor.
It sat there unbroken
until a message swept from eye to eye
embracing its beauty.

Now all goods and distraction are packed away,
leaving the air soft and lightly scented.

When care has been constant and unyielding in a vineyard, one does not find a perfect product, but one with distinct qualities. So it is with people, and such is life. When we care about others and work hard to achieve a worthy purpose, one outside of ourselves, life brings satisfaction, not perfection.

> Ring the bells that still can ring.
> Forget your perfect offering.
> There is a crack in everything.
> That's how the light gets in.
> —Leonard Cohen

2010

The warmth of May 2010 continued straight through the month, except for a scare when the temperature dropped just below freezing one night leaving a hint of frost on the fields that late May morning when our new-growth vine shoots were two to three inches long. While our vines suffered no damage, those of a friend further north were stricken. Fortunately, French hybrid grapes seem to tolerate such events, and even produce new growth again if frost damage occurs. Then, summer came along steadily with very little rain and lots of sun. Japanese beetles appeared shockingly early but were wonderfully scarce. Maybe this would be a New England Sonoma year!

We netted the grapes early, as they progressed to *veraison* (color change) early. I was concerned about bird invasions (although birds typically wait until the week before we pick, when sugar levels are almost prime, to do their own harvest) including turkeys that had been stumbling through our vineyard with their young.

The very next day after we put up the vineyard netting, Lynn was in the garden when she heard grunting and chomping. She spotted a medium-size black bear, apparently eating grapes as he tugged and pulled at the vines. She backed away slowly until she was close to the house, then darted inside the garage and got into her car, driving it about a hundred feet to the vineyard, directly at the bear, who just kept tearing away the netting. She then drove up and down the rows honking, flashing headlights, and yelling at the bear, who wasn't too impressed initially but finally ambled away.

Netting had done its job! Incredibly, the grapes were hardly damaged, and the durable, heavy gauge netting sustained only a single two-foot hole from the claw work. So the grunting and chomping noises, perceived by Lynn as grape enjoyment and chewing, might have been grunts of frustration from pulling at the net. Evidently the frustration was enough that this bear did not return, as we had anticipated. Nonetheless, Lynn started wearing "bear bells" when in the garden. These are very motion-sensitive little bells that clip onto a belt, jingling easily with virtually any motion, to warn bears and other creatures of one's presence, because bears, we were told, don't want to interact with people.

Bears are not so inclined to attack people unless they are provoked or cannot find their usual sources of food, so being "respectful" and walking away slowly while watching a bear is considered best if you want to avoid a difficult wrestling match. In *Cry of the Kalahari* (10), a young couple, Mark and Cordelia Owens, live harmoniously with African wildlife, including lions and hyenas in their campsite, by treating these creatures with respect. Over time, they recognize the distinct hierarchy in their Botswana wilderness. After lions kill a wildebeest they eat as much as they want, and then allow the brown hyenas to partake. The leopards are allowed to feed next, followed by little jackals, other smaller mammals, and finally birds. Respect for others works.

We found that we could deter deer and turkeys from our vineyard by repeatedly chasing them away, as we had literally staked our territory in the vineyard. Lynn (and the netting) let the bear know that he or she was intruding into *our* territory. In this setting, we are the dominant ones, and, like the hyena approaching a kill when the lion is feeding, a bear, a deer, or a turkey will find that he or she is not welcome in our vineyard.

And so we proceeded on to harvest in the second week of September. This glorious day brought together neighbors and friends as well as our son and his friends Matt and Molly. After a mini triathlon, they joined our picking, crushing, and pressing. Lynn, Marcia, and Barbara put together an astounding

Tuscan lunch that we all shared while overlooking the vineyard and sipping a bit of the 2009 vintage.

The sunshine of 2009 had worked! Sugar levels (brix) were at 20–22 for the Saint Croix—well above the levels of previous years, and acid levels were, as expected, concomitantly lower. With Mike and Becky, we picked the white grapes two weeks later, since their sugar was slower to rise and they needed a little more time. All of the juice was sweet and aromatic, leaving great hope for the quality of wine in 2010.

PREFERENCES

We are fortunate, in the cool northwestern corner of Connecticut, to grow wine grapes. The French-American hybrids we grow make good wine, and occasionally we can produce a wine that is really good, but these grapes are very different from *vinifera* grown in Bordeaux or Napa. Connecticut winters are too cold and the growing seasons too short for most *vinifera*, including cabernet sauvignon. Even great soil in the winds and snows of Connecticut cannot produce a meaningful harvest of such warm-weather varietals. The growing seasons are just too short, and the vines are not sturdy enough to handle such winters. Cabernet sauvignon needs long, warm growing seasons to develop the high brix and complexity necessary to yield a wine considered by experienced tasters to be "great." Cabernet, chardonnay, and pinot noir grown in northwest Connecticut can't compare to the same grapes grown in the Burgundy region of France, in Chile, or in the Willamette Valley of Oregon.

Fortunately for short-season growers, the Cayuga grapes that grow well in New England and Upstate New York need to be harvested at a somewhat lower brix, as previously mentioned, in order to make optimal wine. Otherwise, the Cayuga wine may develop "off" flavors. Cayuga is a fantastic grape to grow in cooler climates, and can yield wonderful white wines despite the shorter growing seasons that are tough for optimal cabernet. Even though grape growers in Southern California can grow Cayuga, they stay with *vinifera* grapes like chardonnay and sauvignon blanc, understanding that these grape types produce a better wine in that setting. Some grape types are simply stronger and more resilient than others in certain environments. Some can survive brief winter temperatures of negative thirty degrees (Fahrenheit), while others are irreparably damaged at negative twenty. Some get mildew infections quickly and require more protective sprays, while others, like the hardy American *lambrusca* Concord grape, will grow on trees in a forest and produce grapes, infection-free year after year, without any spray. I have never, though, tasted a Concord grape wine that I would call "great." Marechal Foch grows well in a cooler climate, and cannot rival cabernet for flavor and overall quality of wine, but harvested early at a brix of 18 and then made as a rose wine (fermented off the skins) using GRE yeast, it yields a flavorful and enjoyable blush wine with, perhaps, a little hint of cotton candy scent!

We were watching Momix, a modern-dance group directed by Moses Pendleton, one evening at a fundraiser, and I was struck by the focused athleticism and vigor of the young dancers. Their grace and strength produced a performance that was breathtakingly elegant. I have not generally gone out of my way to attend dance performances, but this was an experience of dance that far exceeded my expectations. It was extraordinary! I thought of people I have known and recalled a psychiatrist friend of mine who told me that his little eight-year-old son was passionate about dancing, and had no interest in ice hockey or soccer like some of the other boys in their neighborhood. Being a psychiatrist, he realized that there was something relatively "hardwired" in his son that was taking him in this direction, and my friend was not going to interfere. His son would, hopefully, thrive as a dancer. Like a young cabernet sauvignon vine that needs lots of sun, air and the terroir of Bordeaux, Chile, or California in order to thrive, this boy would spend much of his youth in dance class to be what he was best suited to be.

We were fortunate to hear the performance of a fourteen-year-old concert pianist playing a concerto with the Vermont Philharmonic orchestra a few years ago. Dressed in a dark suit, he created music that was stunningly powerful. This youngster seemed incongruous playing a magnificent concerto with full orchestra. When he rose from the piano bench to a standing ovation at the conclusion of this impeccably played concerto, he looked like a little kid. We, and many others it seemed, were astonished by his performance and specu-lated, on the way home, about how it must be for a child to spend many hours each day playing the piano. This young man had found the right environment for his abilities. His parents had allowed him to be in the right setting to nur-ture such incredible talent—like chardonnay in Napa.

I thought about another eight-year-old--- son of a friend. The dad is a great tennis player and wanted, more than anything, for his son to play tennis. I watched them playing tennis together and noted that the youngster seemed a bit indifferent. Later, when his dad was talking with someone, I went over to the young boy, who was sitting on the court, pushing around the Har-Tru court topping into little piles. I told him I thought he had some good tennis strokes, and his simple response was, "I don't like tennis." We all know that you can take a horse to water, but you can't make him drink. You can also grow chardonnay in Maine, but the wine won't match up to chardonnay grown in Santa Barbara, California.

I like the experience of drinking wine varietals like chasselas, nebbiolo, Foch, and Cayuga; or a glass of chardonnay aged in steel; and even more than that, a steely, lemony sauvignon blanc or cold Foch fermented off the skins. Each reminds me of the place from which it comes and the people who made it possible, the harvest, and the care that went into its production. Australians love Vegemite and some people like caviar and cognac. Many in France are passionate about goose-liver pâté. Many favor a good piece of cheese and an olive. It all depends on the "palate." No variety wins. No specific region is best. It all depends on preference.

Over time, and as experience grew, we preferred our own wines to many others. We knew their origin. They had been born and raised with loving care, without insecticides. We had grown to appreciate just how good Cayuga, Vidal blanc, Marechal Foch, Saint Croix, and Baco noir can be. We could share them with friends and give them to charitable benefits. We loved to see friends enjoying our best wines.

Love and the Vineyard

Brad had just returned from a vineyard wedding near the tip of Long Island, New York. I asked him his thoughts about why some young couples choose vineyards for their weddings. Brad's first thought was that a vineyard is a "safe" place, one that is interesting and appealing to many people, despite cultural or ethnic differences—a neutral meeting place.

Vineyards are romantic, evoking thoughts of beauty, synchrony, and harmony. Vineyards, for some, are religious, with a comfortable sense, mentioned in the Bible, of unity and connection to higher power. Vineyards are also secular and nonjudgmental. The vines intertwine and coexist comfortably with adjacent vines. A vineyard that is treated well, with careful and accurate trimming, pruning, and weeding, will be prolific, like a good marriage. When two people care for each other, pulling their weeds, letting in light while nurturing each other, their relationship is more likely to succeed. Harmony, light, air, room for growth, attention, respect, kindness, hard work, and caring are no secret in love and wine.

Loving Eyes

Loving eyes, chalice of tenderness—
drinking your tonic, I forget myself
and become ethereal in the warm sun,
my satchel of cares tipped and empty.

The nectar of your voice:
a melody in the air,
dancing like a flower in the wind,
a sensuous tonic
to the soul's sense of eternity.

All creation pauses
at the condensed pleasure
and liquid beauty of your smile,
in a vast moment
like the unified stillness
after a train passes,
leaving one harmony
in the subsequent stillness.

Epilogue

Early in 2017, we invited new neighbors to dinner along with some old friends. I opened bottles of our best 2015 Vidal-Cayuga blend and our favorite full-bodied 2015 Saint Croix. The new neighbors were most curious about the wines and asked questions, as many do, about the process of growing grapes and making wine in Connecticut. These particular wines, however, had benefitted from their origins on older vines, an excellent growing year, and the vintner's sixteen years of experience growing grapes and making wine. They were some of the best we had produced. I noted one of our guests pouring our Saint Croix in preference to a special 1999 Chilean cabernet sauvignon that I had also opened. Somehow, at that moment, it all made sense.

Endnotes

(1)   Thomas, L. *The Lives of a Cell. Notes of a Biology Watcher* (New York: Viking, 1974).

(2)   Arroyo-Garcia, R. "Multiple origins of cultivated grapevine (*Vitis vinifera* L. ssp. *sativa*) based on chloroplast DNA polymorphisms" *Molecular Ecology* 15, no. 12 (October 2006): 3707–14.

(3)   Copley, R.J. "Millions of Bacterial Species Revealed Underfoot," *New Scientist*, August 25, 2005.

(4)   Bishop Andrew Smith in the April–May 2001 *Good News* publication of the Episcopal Diocese of Connecticut.

(5)   Feiring, A. *The Battle for Wine and Love* (Orlando: Mariner Books, 2009).

(6)   Spaziani, G., *The Home Winemaker's Companion* (Pownal, VT: Storey Books, 2000).

(7)   Alvord L. and Van Pelt E., *The Scalpel and the Silver Bear,* (New York, NY: A Bantam Book, 1999)

(8)   Nandipati S and Litvan I. Environmental Exposures and Parkinson's Disease. *Int J Environ Res Public Health.* 2016 Sep 3;13(9)

(9)   Leopold, A. *A Sand County Almanac.* Page 261 (New York, Ballantine Books, 1966)

(10)   Owens, M. and Owens, C. *Cry of the Kalahari* (Cornwall, England: Robert Hartnoll Publishers, 1984)

Made in the USA
Middletown, DE
07 July 2017